Embrace Your Emotions: Mastering Emotional Intelligence for a Harmonious Life

Perry L. Davidson

Published by Perry L. Davidson, 2024.

EMBRACE YOUR EMOTIONS: MASTERING EMOTIONAL INTELLIGENCE FOR A HARMONIOUS LIFE

First edition. July 31, 2024.

ISBN: 979-8227722959

Written by Perry L. Davidson.

Also by Perry L. Davidson

Charisma Unlocked: Forge Lasting Bonds and Radiate Influence
Unleashing the Power of Likability and Charisma
The Stoic Compass: Charting a Course to Serenity in the Modern Age
The Eternal Ink: Keeping the Writer's Flame Alive
Unshakeable: The Stoic's Path to Inner Strength and Serenity
Embrace Your Emotions: Mastering Emotional Intelligence for a
Harmonious Life

Table of Contents

Embrace Your Emotions: Mastering Emotional Intelligence for a Harmonious Life

Unlock Improved Relationships and Career Success in Just Months with Clear, Step-by-Step Emotional Intelligence Techniques.

Preface

"*The only way out of the labyrinth of suffering is to forgive.*" — **John Green.**

Welcome to a journey that promises to enhance your understanding of emotions and your ability to interact harmoniously with the world around you. In these pages, you will discover a guide to mastering emotional intelligence tailored to help you foster improved relationships and achieve career success. The purpose of this book is to demystify the concept of emotional intelligence (EI) and provide you with straightforward, step-by-step techniques that are easy to understand and implement.

I was inspired to write this book after observing the struggles and successes of numerous individuals who grappled with understanding their emotions and those of others. Take, for instance, Emily, a bright and ambitious marketing professional whose career seemed stunted due to her difficulty handling feedback and managing stress. Or consider Mark, a recent college graduate overwhelmed by the complexities of new workplace dynamics and social interactions. Their stories are not unique but a testament to the everyday challenges many face in managing emotional landscapes in personal and professional environments.

These narratives drove me to seek classic and contemporary research on emotional intelligence. I delved into the works of psychologists and thought leaders like Daniel Goleman and Travis Bradberry, whose insights into emotional competencies and social skills have significantly shaped our understanding of EI.

This book is designed for individuals at the outset of their personal development journey. Whether you are a young professional like Emily, a recent graduate like Mark, or someone who wishes to navigate life's emotional challenges more effectively, this guide is crafted for you. No prior knowledge of psychology is required; it is just an openness to learn and apply the principles discussed.

I extend my heartfelt gratitude to the countless individuals who shared their experiences with me, my insightful mentors who have guided my understanding of psychology, and the dedicated team that helped bring this book to life. Your stories, support, and collaboration have been invaluable.

By reading this book, you are taking a significant step toward personal growth and emotional mastery. I sincerely hope that the knowledge and strategies in these pages will empower you to lead a more fulfilling and harmonious life.

Thank you for investing your time with me. I invite you to turn the page and begin this transformative journey toward mastering your emotional intelligence, unlocking improved relationships, and achieving greater career success.

Chapter 1: The Emotional Blueprint: Unlocking Your Inner Intelligence

The cool morning breeze whispered through the open windows of Sarah's small yet cozy apartment, stirring the curtains into a gentle dance. It was early, yet the city outside still rubbed sleep from its eyes with the soft glow of dawn. Sarah sat at her modest kitchen table, a steaming mug of coffee cradled in her hands. She gazed out the window, lost in thought.

Today marked six months since she started her job at a bustling marketing firm downtown—a job she had once thought was her dream. But dreams can change their shapes, much like clouds on a breezy day. Recently, Sarah had been feeling disconnected, not just from her job but also from her colleagues. It wasn't the tasks that drained her; it was something deeper, something more personal.

Her thoughts drifted back to last week's meeting, where she stumbled through a presentation. Her ideas were solid; she knew that much. But conveying them with confidence had been a struggle. She remembered watching her manager's barely concealed impatience and her colleague's sympathetic glances.

That night, she lay awake pondering every moment of that meeting.

It wasn't until she stumbled upon an article about emotional intelligence (EI) that Sarah began to see things differently. The article described EI as the ability to understand and manage one's own emotions and recognize those of others—a skill crucial not just for professional success but also for personal fulfillment.

Intrigued, Sarah spent days absorbing everything she could find on the subject. She learned the key components: self-awareness, self-management, social awareness, and relationship management. Each element opened new insights into how she interacted with herself and others.

As she sipped her coffee, reflecting on these concepts, Sarah realized how unaware she had been of her emotions during that presentation. Fear had gripped her so tightly that it silenced her usual creativity and poise. With this newfound understanding came a plan—to observe herself more closely in moments of stress and to practice regulating these reactions.

The sun crested above the skyline, spilling light across the room and casting long shadows on the floor beside her chair. This light seemed to fill Sarah with warmth and clarity.

She set down her mug and smiled slightly at how simple yet profound this revelation felt—knowing oneself deeply could transform every interaction one had and turn routine exchanges into moments of connection and understanding.

As Sarah prepared for another day at work armed with this insight into emotional intelligence, one might wonder: Could mastering these skills truly bridge the gap between merely coping in life's roles and thriving within them?

Discover the Key to a More Fulfilling Life and Career

Emotional intelligence (EI) is not just a beneficial skill set; it's a fundamental aspect of achieving success and fulfillment in both personal and professional realms. As we delve into this journey of emotional mastery, we begin by exploring the foundational concept of EI, its significance, and its transformative potential through real-life examples. This chapter sets the stage for a profound understanding of how emotional intelligence can be your most powerful tool in navigating life's challenges and opportunities.

The narrative of Sarah, a recent graduate stepping into the complex world of professional environments and personal relationships, serves as an illustrative guide throughout this exploration. Her story is not unique but a universal testament to many's struggles in understanding and managing their emotions effectively. By highlighting her experiences, we aim to demystify the practical applications of emotional intelligence in everyday situations.

EI encompasses more than just managing one's emotions; it extends to recognizing and influencing the emotions of others.

This ability is crucial for building healthier relationships, achieving career goals, and maintaining personal well-being. The chapter will outline the core components of emotional intelligence—self-awareness, self-management, social awareness, and relationship management—and discuss their role in enhancing life quality.

Through Sarah's journey, readers will see firsthand how developing skills like empathy, self-regulation, and effective communication can significantly improve various aspects of life. These transformations are not only about achieving external success but also about fostering internal growth and resilience.

As we move forward, this chapter will not only define emotional intelligence but also provide a clear pathway to harnessing its benefits. *It's about turning introspective insights into outward successes,* transforming theoretical knowledge into practical achievements.

The Broad Spectrum of Emotional Intelligence

Understanding emotional intelligence requires us to examine the micro and macro aspects of how emotions operate within and in our interactions with others. This dual perspective ensures that EI is not seen merely as a personal tool for self-improvement but as a bridge to better societal interactions and professional networks.

Moreover, the integration of emotional intelligence into daily life speaks directly to those who are looking to enhance their interpersonal dynamics and professional efficacy without sacrificing their personal happiness and mental health.

Empowering Through Emotional Clarity

By embracing emotional intelligence, individuals empower themselves with the clarity needed to navigate life's complexities with greater ease and confidence. Each section of this chapter builds upon the last, crafting a comprehensive picture that encourages continuous personal development.

In essence, this chapter lays down the emotional blueprint that every reader can use to construct a more harmonious life. It's an invitation to transform passive awareness into active mastery, ensuring that each step taken is informed by empathy, controlled by self-awareness, directed by effective relationship management, and enriched by social awareness.

This exploration is just the beginning. As you progress through the book, each chapter builds on these concepts, providing a robust framework for understanding and applying emotional intelligence in all facets of life. By mastering these skills, you set yourself up for success and lasting happiness—professionally and personally.

Emotional intelligence, often called EI or EQ, is the ability to effectively recognize and manage emotions in oneself and others. It encompasses a range of skills crucial for personal success and fulfillment in various aspects of life, including relationships, career, and overall well-being. ***Understanding emotional intelligence is not just about knowing what emotions are; it's about navigating them skillfully.*** This means being aware of your feelings, regulating them appropriately, empathizing with others, and handling interpersonal relationships tactfully and empathetically.

The significance of emotional intelligence in personal success cannot be overstated. Individuals with high emotional intelligence tend to have stronger social skills, better conflict-resolution abilities, and enhanced communication prowess. These qualities are invaluable in both personal and professional settings. *People with high emotional intelligence often excel in leadership roles, are more adaptable to change, and have greater self-awareness.* They can easily navigate complex social dynamics, build strong relationships, and inspire trust and confidence in others.

Emotional intelligence also plays a crucial role in personal fulfillment. When you understand your emotions and those of others, you can foster deeper connections, cultivate empathy, and create a more harmonious environment. *Having a high level of emotional intelligence allows you to lead a more authentic and purposeful life*, aligning your actions with your values and goals. It enables you to make informed decisions based on rational thinking and emotional insights.

Honing your emotional intelligence skills can unlock a world of possibilities for personal growth and fulfillment. Whether you're aiming for career advancement, seeking healthier relationships, or striving for inner peace, emotional intelligence is the key to success on multiple fronts. *Embracing emotional intelligence is not just about managing emotions; it's about harnessing them as a source of strength and wisdom.* When you learn to tap into the power of emotions intelligently, you pave the way for a more enriching life experience.

Please keep reading to discover how Sarah's journey unfolds as she unlocks the transformative potential of emotional intelligence in her personal and professional life.

Sarah's journey with emotional intelligence began when she entered the workforce after graduating from college. She quickly realized that academic achievements alone were not enough to thrive in a professional setting. Despite her technical skills, she needed help navigating office politics, communicating effectively with colleagues, and managing the stress of tight deadlines and demanding clients. Frustrated with her lack of progress and feeling overwhelmed by the demands of her job, Sarah knew she needed to make a change.

DISCOVERING EMOTIONAL Intelligence

In her quest for self-improvement, Sarah stumbled upon the concept of emotional intelligence (EI). Intrigued by the idea that success in both personal and professional realms hinges on more than just cognitive abilities, she delved into understanding how emotions shape interactions and outcomes. Through self-reflection and introspection, Sarah uncovered a wealth of insights about her emotional responses and their impact on her relationships and performance at work.

Transformative Impact

As Sarah began to apply the principles of emotional intelligence in her daily life, she noticed a profound transformation. Honing her self-awareness gave her valuable insights into her strengths, weaknesses, and triggers. This newfound awareness empowered her to regulate emotions more effectively, improving decision-making and conflict-resolution skills. In interactions with colleagues, Sarah demonstrated greater empathy and social awareness, fostering stronger connections and more collaborative relationships.

Balancing Personal and Professional Life

The benefits of emotional intelligence extended beyond the workplace for Sarah. By developing her ability to manage relationships and navigate social dynamics with finesse, she also experienced a positive shift in her personal life. Communication with friends and family became more open and authentic, deepening bonds and fostering a sense of belonging. Sarah's newfound emotional intelligence enhanced her professional success and enriched her overall well-being.

Embracing Growth Opportunities

Through Sarah's story, we witness the immense potential for personal growth that emotional intelligence offers. By embracing EI principles such as self-management, social awareness, and relationship management, individuals can unlock their inner intelligence and harness it to achieve success in various aspects of life. Sarah's journey serves as a testament to the transformative power of emotional intelligence in shaping one's destiny and creating a harmonious balance between professional achievements and personal fulfillment.

Navigating Challenges with Emotional Intelligence

Sarah's experiences highlight the importance of resilience in the face of challenges. By cultivating emotional intelligence, individuals can build the strength to overcome obstacles, adapt to change, and thrive in diverse environments. The ability to navigate setbacks with grace and composure is a hallmark of high emotional intelligence, empowering individuals like Sarah to turn adversities into opportunities for growth and learning.

The Key Components of Emotional Intelligence

Understanding the core components of emotional intelligence—self-awareness, self-management, social awareness, and relationship management—provides a roadmap for personal development and success. These pillars form the foundation upon which individuals can build strong interpersonal skills, effective communication strategies, and robust emotional resilience. By mastering these key components, individuals like Sarah can unlock their full potential and lead fulfilling lives marked by meaningful connections and professional achievements.

Emotional intelligence is not just a buzzword; it is a powerful tool that can shape our interactions with others, influence our decision-making processes, and ultimately determine our levels of success and satisfaction in life. Through Sarah's journey, we learn that emotional intelligence is attainable and essential for navigating modern life's complexities with confidence and grace.

Emotional intelligence consists of critical components vital in enhancing the quality of life. *Self-awareness* is the foundation on which emotional intelligence is built. It involves understanding one's emotions, strengths, weaknesses, values, and goals. With self-awareness, it becomes easier to navigate the complexities of emotions effectively. *Self-management* is regulating one's feelings and behaviors in different situations. This component allows individuals to stay composed under pressure, adapt to change, and control impulses effectively.

Social awareness is another crucial aspect of emotional intelligence. It involves recognizing and understanding the emotions of others, empathizing with them, and navigating social dynamics adeptly. By being attuned to the feelings and needs of those around us, we can build stronger relationships and foster a sense of connection. *Relationship management* is the final piece of the emotional intelligence puzzle. It encompasses communicating clearly, resolving conflicts constructively, inspiring and influencing others positively, and working collaboratively towards common goals.

Each component of emotional intelligence contributes uniquely to enhancing life quality. *Self-awareness* enables individuals to make informed decisions aligned with their values and aspirations. *Self-management empowers* individuals to respond thoughtfully rather than impulsively in challenging situations, leading to better outcomes and reduced stress levels. *Social awareness* fosters empathy and compassion, nurturing deeper connections with others and promoting a sense of belonging.

Relationship management, the most outwardly focused component, allows individuals to cultivate harmonious interactions with colleagues, friends, family members, and partners. By honing these skills, individuals can build trust, resolve conflicts peacefully, and create supportive environments where everyone can thrive. The synergy between these components creates a robust framework for navigating life's complexities with grace and emotional resilience.

In essence, emotional intelligence is a compass that guides individuals toward fulfilling relationships, successful careers, and overall well-being. By developing these essential components—self-awareness, self-management, social awareness, and relationship management—we equip ourselves with invaluable tools for personal growth and professional success. Through intentional practice and reflection on these components, individuals can unlock their inner intelligence and harness the power of emotional intelligence to lead more enriching lives filled with authentic connections and meaningful achievements.

Emotional intelligence (EI) is a cornerstone of professional achievement and personal satisfaction. Through the exploration of its fundamental aspects and Sarah's inspiring journey, we've uncovered the profound influence EI can exert on an individual's life. Sarah's story exemplifies how cultivating skills such as self-awareness, self-management, social awareness, and relationship management can substantially improve various life domains.

Understanding and developing EI is about navigating workplace dynamics and enhancing personal relationships and overall mental well-being. As we've seen, empathizing with others, managing one's emotions, and fostering positive interactions is invaluable.

These skills empower individuals to face challenges with resilience, adapt to changes flexibly, and engage with others more effectively.

The rewards for anyone stepping into the realm of emotional intelligence are multifaceted. By integrating the core components of EI into their daily lives, they open doors *to **enhanced communication, stronger relationships, and increased confidence***. These benefits not only propel them towards career success but also enrich their personal experiences, leading to a more fulfilled and harmonious life.

As you continue through this book, each chapter will build on the foundation, offering practical strategies and deeper insights into mastering your emotional landscape. You are embarking on a transformative journey that promises to ***equip you with the tools needed for personal growth and professional excellence.***

Embrace the lessons from Sarah's transformation and the insights shared about the pivotal role of emotional intelligence. Let these guide you as you navigate your path toward becoming more emotionally intelligent. The journey ahead is exciting and rich with potential for growth—both in your inner world and your interactions with the world around you.

Chapter 2: Beyond Feelings: The Art of Emotional Application

In the dim light of early morning, Anna sat at the edge of her bed, her mind as turbulent as the gusts rattling the windowpanes. Today was not just another day; it was the day she would confront her manager about the overlooked promotion, a scenario that demanded courage and keen emotional intelligence. The room was still, filled with the soft hum of a city awakening and the distant barks of a restless dog. She felt the weight of her decision pressing down upon her like the heavy quilts piled atop her lap.

Anna's thoughts drifted to last week's meeting—the tight smiles, the quick nods, barely disguising indifference. She remembered how her ideas had dissolved into the murmurs of afterthoughts among her colleagues. It wasn't just about being heard but about feeling seen and recognized. As she sipped her lukewarm coffee, its bitterness mirrored her internal unrest. This wasn't just about a job; it was about respect and acknowledgment.

She pondered over how emotional intelligence could guide her actions today. Understanding her manager's perspectives and emotions could be crucial. Was he under pressure from his superiors? Or perhaps he is unaware of his biases? Anna knew that recognizing these subtleties could turn the tide in her favor.

With each step towards work, she rehearsed what she would say, tuning into each emotion that surfaced—fear, hope, determination—and channeling them into a calm resolve. The city around her moved briskly: cars honked impatiently while cyclists weaved through traffic like a thread through the fabric. The chill in the air bit into her cheeks, sharpening her senses and resolve.

As she entered the office building, its familiar smells—waxed floors and brewed coffee—grounded her swirling thoughts. She greeted coworkers with a practiced smile but was acutely aware of their moods and tensions—a skill she had honed over the years but only recently understood its power in navigating workplace dynamics.

Will understanding and managing emotions be enough for Anna to change how others view her and how they value her contributions?

Harnessing Emotional Wisdom for Life Mastery

Emotional intelligence (EI) is often misunderstood as merely the capacity to identify one's emotions and those of others. However, it extends far beyond this basic understanding, encompassing a sophisticated skill set that strategically applies *these insights to* enhance personal and professional interactions. This chapter delves into the depths of EI, exploring how it can transform mere feelings into actionable wisdom that propels us towards more fulfilling relationships and successful career paths.

At its core, emotional intelligence offers us the tools to *navigate complex social landscapes* with grace and effectiveness. By understanding the multifaceted nature of emotions, we equip ourselves with the ability to respond rather than react—a subtle yet profound shift in behavior management. This approach improves our interpersonal relationships and amplifies our decision-making capabilities.

The Multifaceted Nature of Emotional Intelligence

Emotional intelligence is not a monolithic skill but a composite of several competencies that include self-awareness, emotional regulation, empathy, motivation, and social skills. Each component is crucial in how we perceive and interact with the world.

Understanding these elements provides a foundation for discussing how emotions can be harnessed to foster better decisions and behaviors.

Strategic Application of Emotions

Imagine assessing a heated situation with clarity and precision, using your emotional insight to guide your actions rather than letting raw feelings dictate your response. This chapter will explore practical strategies for applying emotional knowledge effectively, ensuring that emotions serve as tools for enhancement rather than obstacles to success.

Impact on Actions and Outcomes

The ripple effects of developed emotional intelligence are profound. They extend into every corner of our lives—from enhancing leadership skills and conflict resolution to deepening personal relationships and self-understanding. We will examine diverse scenarios where high emotional intelligence provides a distinct advantage, illustrating its importance in everyday situations and long-term achievements.

Through this exploration, you will discover that mastering emotional intelligence is about achieving immediate goals and cultivating a life of harmony and understanding. It's about transforming instinctual reactions into thoughtfully crafted responses that align with our deepest values and aspirations.

In essence, this chapter sets the stage for recognizing that our emotions are not just brief feelings but valuable insights that can lead to significant personal growth and success when understood and applied correctly. By embracing this perspective, we open doors to new possibilities in every realm of life—personal development, professional advancement, and beyond.

By fostering an authentic connection with our emotions and learning how to apply them strategically in various aspects of life, we enhance our own well-being and contribute positively to the communities around us. Let us embark on this journey with open hearts and minds, ready to harness the full potential of our emotional selves.

Emotional intelligence goes far beyond simply recognizing emotions; it encompasses a multifaceted understanding of how emotions work, how they can be used strategically, and how they impact behavior and decision-making. It is not just about identifying feelings in oneself and others; it involves applying emotional knowledge to enhance relationships, navigate social interactions, and achieve personal and professional success.

Understanding Emotional Intelligence: To truly master emotional intelligence, one must delve deeper into the complexities of human emotions. It involves not only recognizing one's own feelings but also comprehending the emotions of others. This understanding forms the foundation for building strong connections, fostering empathy, and improving communication skills. Emotional intelligence is more than just being in touch with one's feelings; it's about using that emotional awareness to guide actions and responses in various situations.

Utilizing Emotional Information: The strategic use of emotions is crucial to emotional intelligence. It involves harnessing emotional data to make informed decisions, solve problems effectively, and manage conflicts constructively. By leveraging emotional information, individuals can enhance their behavior, build stronger relationships, and achieve greater success in both personal and professional endeavors. Emotional intelligence empowers individuals to use their emotions as tools for growth and development rather than allowing them to dictate reactions impulsively.

Managing Emotions Effectively: A crucial aspect of emotional intelligence is skillfully managing emotions. This includes regulating feelings in challenging situations, controlling impulses, and expressing emotions appropriately. By mastering emotional regulation, individuals can avoid unnecessary conflicts, maintain composure under pressure, and make sound judgments based on rational thinking rather than being swayed by volatile emotions.

Emotional intelligence is a dynamic skill that evolves with practice and self-awareness. By honing this skill set, individuals can transform their approach to relationships, decision-making processes, and overall well-being. Developing emotional intelligence requires exploring one's own emotional landscape, engaging with others empathetically, and applying emotional insights strategically in various contexts.

In the next section, dive deeper into the strategic application of emotions to improve behavior and decision-making.

Emotional intelligence goes beyond simply recognizing feelings; it involves strategically using emotions to enhance behavior and decision-making. By understanding the multifaceted nature of emotional intelligence, individuals can harness their emotions effectively to improve various aspects of their lives. *Emotions are a powerful tool that can positively impact behavior and outcomes in personal and professional settings.*

When individuals learn to navigate their emotions strategically, they can improve their relationships, communication, and overall well-being. *By leveraging emotional intelligence, one can make more informed decisions and respond thoughtfully to challenging situations.* Rather than being controlled by emotions, individuals can use them as valuable sources of information to guide their actions.

Emotions are not obstacles to be overcome but tools to be utilized. By recognizing emotions' role in decision-making, individuals can make choices that align with their values and goals. Strategic use of emotions involves being mindful of one's feelings and considering how they influence thoughts and behaviors.

Emotional intelligence enables individuals to regulate their responses, leading to more constructive interactions with others. Individuals can navigate conflicts with greater understanding and compassion through self-awareness and empathy. This emotional agility fosters healthier relationships and enhances collaboration in both personal and professional settings.

By incorporating emotional intelligence into decision-making, individuals can make choices that are not only logical but also emotionally sound. This holistic approach considers cognitive reasoning and emotional insight, leading to more balanced and effective decisions. Emotions provide valuable data that, when integrated strategically, can lead to more authentic and fulfilling outcomes.

Emotional intelligence is a critical factor in enhancing behavior and decision-making. By acknowledging the importance of emotions in daily interactions, individuals can cultivate a greater sense of self-awareness and empathy. This heightened emotional intelligence allows for more intentional responses that align with personal values and long-term goals.

The strategic use of emotions empowers individuals to navigate complex situations with clarity and purpose. By incorporating emotional intelligence into decision-making, individuals can cultivate stronger relationships, make more informed choices, and lead more fulfilling lives.

Emotional intelligence plays a pivotal role in determining the outcomes of our actions in various scenarios. *Understanding and managing emotions effectively* can significantly influence the trajectory of our personal and professional lives. When faced with challenges or conflicts, individuals with high emotional intelligence are better equipped to navigate them successfully. By being aware of their emotions and those of others, individuals can tailor their responses and decisions to achieve more favorable results.

Emotional intelligence impacts communication, which is essential in all aspects of life. Those who excel in emotional intelligence can clearly convey their thoughts and feelings, fostering better understanding and connection with others. This ability to communicate effectively leads to more substantial personal and professional relationships. By recognizing emotions in oneself and others, individuals can adapt their communication style to suit different situations, leading to more positive interactions and outcomes.

Decision-making is another area where emotional intelligence shines. Assessing one's emotions and understanding how they may impact choices allows for more informed and rational decision-making. Emotionally intelligent individuals can separate their feelings from decision-making, leading to more objective and beneficial outcomes. This skill is precious in high-pressure situations where quick, strategic decisions are crucial.

Conflict resolution is inherently linked to emotional intelligence. Those with high emotional intelligence can navigate conflicts gracefully and tactfully, seeking resolutions that benefit all parties involved. By managing emotions effectively during disagreements or misunderstandings, individuals can de-escalate tense situations and find common ground for peaceful resolutions. This ability preserves relationships and fosters a culture of understanding and collaboration.

Emotional intelligence greatly enhances leadership effectiveness. Leaders who understand their emotions and their team members' emotions can inspire trust, motivation, and loyalty. Empathizing with others' perspectives and needs, emotionally intelligent leaders create a supportive environment that encourages growth and success. Their ability to manage emotions under pressure sets a positive example for their team, leading to higher productivity and job satisfaction.

Emotional intelligence acts as a shield against impulsive reactions or negative behaviors in stressful situations. Individuals with high emotional intelligence can maintain composure under stress, making calculated decisions rather than succumbing to heightened emotions. This resilience enables them to face challenges head-on, finding solutions not clouded by temporary feelings but guided by long-term objectives.

Overall, emotional intelligence guides various scenarios, shaping our actions and profoundly influencing outcomes. By honing this skill through self-awareness, empathy, effective communication, and conflict-resolution strategies, individuals can navigate life's complexities with confidence and grace. The impact of emotional intelligence extends far beyond personal interactions; it is a crucial ingredient for success in relationships and careers.

Emotional intelligence (EI) is more than an academic concept; it's a practical tool that, when mastered, can transform our interactions and decision-making processes. Throughout this chapter, we've explored how emotional intelligence extends beyond simply recognizing feelings. It involves understanding, using, and managing emotions to enhance our behavior and the quality of our relationships.

Understanding the multifaceted nature of EI is crucial. It empowers us to grasp our own emotional landscapes and decipher the emotional states of others around us. This insight is invaluable, as it influences how we react in various situations—be it at home, in social settings, or in the workplace.

Another critical aspect of emotional intelligence is the strategic use of emotions to guide our behavior and decision-making. By consciously applying what we know about emotions, we can make more informed choices aligned with our goals and values. This strategic application helps us navigate challenges more effectively and achieve better outcomes.

Moreover, examining ***how emotional intelligence affects actions and outcomes*** in different scenarios has revealed its pervasive impact. Whether resolving conflicts, fostering teamwork, or leading with empathy, EI is a cornerstone of successful interactions and leadership.

Emotional intelligence is not just about personal gain; it contributes to a harmonious life. It equips us with the skills to handle interpersonal relationships judiciously and empathetically, enhancing personal and professional aspects of our lives.

Moving forward, let's embrace these insights and continue to cultivate our emotional intelligence. By doing so, we improve our lives and contribute to a more emotionally intelligent and understanding world. Remember, the journey of enhancing EI is ongoing and consistently rewarding. Let's commit to this path of growth and discovery, ensuring that each step we take is informed by empathy, strategic thinking, and a deep understanding of human emotions.

Chapter 3: The Core Quartet: Building Blocks of Emotional Mastery

Elena walked along the bustling streets of downtown, the sounds of the city humming like a restless sea around her. The late afternoon sun cast long shadows over the pavement, and people brushed past their own worlds, their own crises. She clutched her coffee close, feeling its warmth seep through the cardboard, a small comfort against the chill that had started to cut through her coat.

She was thinking about the meeting she had just left. It was supposed to be a routine project discussion, but it had spiraled quickly when tempers flared. Jack's voice still rang in her ears—sharp, accusing. She could feel her heartbeat quicken at the memory; she felt cornered and misunderstood. Elena knew she should've handled it better. But how? Her mind circled back to self-awareness and self-management, those cornerstones of emotional intelligence she'd read about but struggled to practice in such moments.

As she turned a corner, her thoughts were interrupted by a street musician's melancholic violin strains spilling into the air, weaving through the noise of traffic and chatter. She paused for a moment to listen. The music spoke of sorrow but also carried a thread of resilience that lifted Elena's spirits slightly.

Social awareness and relationship management—the words floated back to her as she watched an elderly couple pause by the musician, dropping some coins into his open violin case with gentle smiles. They shared an understanding glance with him that spoke volumes about empathy and connection without exchanging words.

Elena thought about her team and Jack and wondered what lay beneath his outburst today. Had she missed signs of his stress? Could understanding his perspective more deeply help them move forward together more effectively?

She resumed walking, letting these questions simmer as she navigated through crowds of people crossing an intersection. The crowd pushed forward in waves under fading light; everyone absorbed in their little dramas.

What if Elena could master these emotional skills? Would it change how she felt now? Would it change how others responded to her? As night began to fold around the city's shoulders like a dark shawl, Elena felt daunted and intrigued by these possibilities. What would happen if we all understood just a little better, not only our emotions but those of others around us?

Unlock the Pillars of Emotional Mastery

Emotional Intelligence (EI) is not just a buzzword—it's a transformative tool that can dramatically enhance how we perceive, engage with, and respond to the world around us. The four core competencies of ***self-awareness, self-management, social awareness, and relationship management*** are the heart of this transformative journey. These are not just abstract concepts, but practical skills that can be developed to improve personal effectiveness and interpersonal relations. This chapter delves into these foundational elements, setting the stage for a journey toward emotional mastery that can inspire and motivate you to reach your full potential.

The Foundation: Self-Awareness and Self-Management

Understanding and managing our own emotions are the most crucial steps in developing emotional intelligence. ***Self-awareness allows*** us to recognize our feelings and the triggers that elicit them, providing a deeper insight into our intrinsic motivations and reactions. For instance, when you feel anxious before a presentation, acknowledging this emotion can help you prepare better. Coupled with ***self-management,*** which empowers us to control and adapt our emotions to various situations, these skills form the bedrock of personal emotional regulation. For example, when a colleague criticizes your work, self-management can help you respond calmly and constructively. Through engaging narratives and real-life applications, we will explore how these skills benefit personal well-being and enhance our decision-making processes.

Beyond the Self: Social Awareness and Relationship Management

Moving beyond personal mastery, emotional intelligence extends its reach into how we perceive and interact with others. *Social awareness* involves recognizing and understanding the emotions of those around us, an essential skill in navigating complex social landscapes. *Relationship management*, on the other hand, leverages this understanding to foster successful interactions and build meaningful relationships. This chapter will illuminate how these competencies are critical in personal and professional life, influencing leadership styles, team dynamics, and conflict resolution.

Understanding these four core skills provides a framework for enhancing emotional intelligence, but integrating them requires practice and mindfulness. Each section of this chapter will introduce practical strategies that aid in cultivating these abilities, emphasizing the importance of continuous growth and learning. By making these strategies practical and applicable to your daily life, you will feel empowered and ready to harness the full potential of your emotional capabilities.

By embracing these core competencies, individuals can achieve a more harmonious life, marked by improved relationships and career success. The journey through emotional intelligence is a profound transformation that begins with self-understanding but extends far beyond oneself.

This introduction sets the stage for a deeper exploration of these areas. As we progress, remember that developing proficiency in these skills is a dynamic process that enriches individual lives and the communities they touch. Join us as we unpack these concepts further, providing you with the tools needed to harness the full potential of your emotional capabilities. Now, it's your turn to apply these concepts in your daily life. Start by practicing self-awareness and self-management in your interactions with others. We look forward to hearing about your experiences and the positive changes you've noticed.

Emotional intelligence comprises four fundamental skills that are the building blocks for mastering one's emotions and interactions with others. *Self-awareness* is the first cornerstone, enabling individuals to recognize and understand their emotions. It involves attuning to one's feelings, thoughts, and behaviors without judgment. *Self-management follows* closely, allowing individuals to regulate and control their feelings effectively. This skill empowers individuals to respond rather than react impulsively to situations, fostering emotional balance and resilience.

Social awareness is the third critical skill in emotional intelligence, emphasizing the importance of understanding others' emotions and perspectives. It involves empathy, compassion, and the ability to pick up on non-verbal cues to comprehend how others are feeling. Lastly, *relationship management* encapsulates utilizing self-awareness, self-management, and social awareness to cultivate successful interactions with others. This skill involves effective communication, conflict resolution, and collaboration to build strong and harmonious relationships.

These four core emotional intelligence skills are essential for personal growth, successful relationships, and career advancement. They form the foundation upon which individuals can navigate the complexities of human emotions with grace and understanding.

Each skill complements the others, creating a holistic framework for emotional mastery. This comprehensive journey of self-improvement fosters well-being and fulfillment in various aspects of life, making you feel that you are on the right path to personal and professional success.

By developing self-awareness, individuals can gain clarity on their emotions and behaviors, leading to better decision-making and increased self-confidence. Self-management enables individuals to handle stressors effectively, maintain composure in challenging situations, and exhibit self-control when faced with adversity. Social awareness allows individuals to connect with others on a deeper level, fostering empathy, compassion, and stronger interpersonal relationships. Relationship management equips individuals with the tools to navigate conflicts constructively, communicate assertively yet empathetically, and build trust with others.

Delve deeper into each core skill of emotional intelligence to unlock your full potential in understanding and managing your emotions effectively.

Self-awareness and self-management are two fundamental pillars in the realm of emotional intelligence. *Self-awareness* **involves** recognizing and understanding one's emotions, strengths, weaknesses, values, and goals. It is the ability to introspect and grasp how emotions can impact thoughts, behaviors, and interactions with others. By honing this skill, individuals can enhance their capacity for empathy and improve their relationships.

Conversely, self-management pertains to regulating emotions, thoughts, and behaviors in different situations. This skill enables individuals to stay composed under pressure, adapt to changing circumstances, and make sound decisions even in challenging scenarios.

The impact of self-awareness on personal emotional regulation cannot be overstated. When individuals are attuned to their emotions and triggers, they are better equipped to navigate life's complexities gracefully and with composure. Understanding one's emotional landscape allows for more authentic self-expression and fosters a deeper connection with others. Acknowledging feelings without judgment or suppression can cultivate inner peace and resilience.

Similarly, *self-management* plays a crucial role in maintaining emotional balance and well-being. Individuals can navigate conflicts effectively and foster healthier relationships by developing the ability to manage impulses, control reactions, and adapt to various situations constructively. Self-management empowers individuals to respond thoughtfully rather than impulsively, leading to more positive outcomes in both personal and professional spheres.

In essence, *self-awareness* provides the foundation for emotional intelligence by offering insights into one's inner world. Self-management is the practical application of these insights in real-life scenarios. These skills form a powerful combination that enables individuals to regulate their emotions effectively, communicate assertively yet empathetically, and make decisions aligned with their values and goals.

By consistently cultivating self-awareness and practicing self-management, individuals can enhance their emotional intelligence and positively transform their lives. These skills contribute to personal growth and lay the groundwork for building meaningful relationships based on trust, respect, and mutual understanding.

Embracing self-awareness and self-management is not merely about controlling emotions but about harnessing them as tools for personal development and interpersonal effectiveness.

Emotional Mastery Matrix Framework

The *Emotional Mastery Matrix framework* guides understanding and enhancing the four core emotional intelligence skills: self-awareness, self-management, social awareness, and relationship management. This model consists of a two-dimensional grid that categorizes behaviors and actions based on their level of competency in each skill area. By visualizing where one falls within the matrix, individuals can identify their strengths and areas for improvement, leading to targeted development strategies tailored to their unique starting point.

Self-Awareness & Management Quadrant

In this quadrant, individuals focus on recognizing and regulating their own emotions. *Self-awareness* involves understanding one's emotions, strengths, weaknesses, values, and goals. It allows individuals to recognize how emotions impact thoughts and behavior. *Conversely, self-management* is the ability to control impulses, manage stress, adapt to changing circumstances, and maintain a positive outlook. Individuals in this quadrant excel at understanding their emotional landscape and effectively managing their reactions.

Social Awareness & Relationship Management Quadrant

The *social awareness* and *relationship management* quadrant is on the matrix's flip side. **Social awareness** involves empathy, organizational awareness, and service orientation - the ability to understand others' emotions, needs, and concerns. It allows individuals to navigate social dynamics effectively and build meaningful connections. *Relationship management* focuses on inspiring others, influencing others effectively, developing others, managing conflicts, and building bonds. Individuals in this quadrant excel at leveraging their understanding of emotions to foster positive relationships with those around them.

Interactions Within the Framework

The *Emotional Mastery Matrix* emphasizes the interconnected nature of these four core emotional intelligence skills. Each quadrant relies on the others for comprehensive emotional mastery. For instance, strong self-awareness can lead to more effective social awareness by providing a solid foundation for understanding one's emotions before interpreting others'. Similarly, effective relationship management can enhance self-management by providing opportunities for practice in real-world interactions.

Dynamics of the Model

Individuals can move within the matrix over time and with deliberate practice as they develop their emotional intelligence skills. The framework encourages continual self-evaluation and growth by offering specific behavioral indicators and actionable steps for improvement within each quadrant. By striving for balance across all four skills, individuals can enhance their emotional intelligence and improve their interpersonal relationships.

Practical Implications

The ***Emotional Mastery Matrix*** provides a practical roadmap for individuals seeking to enhance their emotional intelligence. By identifying where they fall within the matrix and targeting specific areas for improvement, individuals can make tangible progress in developing crucial skills for personal and professional success. The framework offers clear guidance on how to cultivate self-awareness, self-management, social awareness, and relationship management in a structured and actionable manner.

In summary, the ***Emotional Mastery Matrix*** offers a structured approach to developing emotional intelligence by highlighting the importance of self-awareness, self-management, social awareness, and relationship management. By understanding how these core skills interact within the framework and applying targeted strategies for improvement, individuals can enhance their emotional mastery over time.

In mastering ***Emotional Intelligence (EI)***, the core quartet of self-awareness, self-management, social awareness, and relationship management proves indispensable. These building blocks foster personal growth and enhance interactions in every sphere of life. This chapter has laid a foundation, illustrating how each skill interlinks to form a robust framework for emotional mastery.

Self-awareness and self-management are crucial in regulating one's emotions, paving the way for a balanced life. Recognizing and managing our feelings helps in mitigating stress and making informed decisions.

Conversely, *social awareness and relationship management* extend these insights outward, improving our understanding of others and nurturing healthier relationships. Together, these skills create a synergy that amplifies personal and professional successes.

Step-by-Step Process: Cultivating Core Awareness for Emotional Mastery

Enhancing self-awareness involves intentional practices integrating reflection, observation, feedback, and emotional labeling. Each step designed here is actionable and structured to progressively deepen your understanding of your emotional landscape.

Step 1: Reflect on Personal Experiences

Allocate moments to ponder past experiences. Identifying the emotions involved and their impact on one's behavior is crucial. Regularly jotting these reflections in a journal aids in recognizing emotional patterns.

Step 2: Practice Mindful Observation

Dedicate daily time for mindfulness. Observing thoughts and feelings in a non-judgmental space helps pinpoint emotional triggers and understand their origins. Documenting these observations will provide insights over time.

STEP 3: SEEK FEEDBACK

Engaging with close contacts for constructive feedback on your emotional responses can unveil blind spots in self-perception. Embrace this feedback to refine your understanding of how you are perceived emotionally.

Step 4: Engage in Self-Reflection

Deepen the practice of self-reflection by exploring the beliefs and values that shape your emotional responses. Understanding the 'why' behind your feelings is pivotal in achieving emotional clarity.

Step 5: Practice Emotional Labeling

Cultivate the habit of naming your emotions as they arise. Accurately describing feelings enhances communication and assists in emotional regulation.

Step 6: Seek Professional Help if Needed

If emotional challenges become overwhelming, seeking professional advice is a wise step. Therapists can provide tailored strategies that are effective in navigating complex emotional landscapes.

This structured approach equips you with tools to enhance self-awareness and empowers you to manage your emotions adeptly. Investing time in these practices leads to emotional mastery, ensuring a more fulfilled and harmonious life.

Embracing these foundational skills of EI does more than improve individual well-being; it fosters a compassionate, understanding society where meaningful connections thrive. As we continue exploring Emotional Intelligence's nuances in subsequent chapters, remember that each step taken in developing these core skills significantly enriches both personal growth and social interactions.

Chapter 4: Cultivating Growth: Practical Strategies for Emotional Enhancement

In the muted light of a late afternoon, Thomas walked through the bustling city park, his hands buried in the pockets of his worn jacket. Leaves rustled underfoot, whispering secrets to the wind as he passed. His mind was a tumultuous sea, waves crashing against thoughts of tomorrow's crucial meeting—his chance to mend fences with a team fractured by miscommunication and unchecked emotions.

He paused beside a quiet pond, watching a mother duck lead her ducklings through ripples that glinted like scattered coins. Thomas remembered his mentor's advice on emotional intelligence: how awareness and empathy could bridge gaps between intent and perception. He had laughed it off then, thinking it nothing more than soft skills fluff. Standing here, he wondered if those simple tools could be the key.

As children shouted nearby, their joy piercing the usual hum of city life, Thomas thought about journaling. He imagined writing down his feelings each night, tracing the contours of his day with words that could help make sense of his reactions and those around him. Could seeing his emotions on paper show him patterns he was blind to?

A breeze stirred the trees above him, sending a cascade of leaves fluttering around him like snowflakes in slow motion. It brought to mind the practice of mindful observation. Focusing on these small beauties might calm his turbulent thoughts and sharpen his focus on what truly mattered in conversations: the words spoken and the silences between them.

Children's laughter faded as they ran off toward new adventures, leaving echoes that filled the space with lingering warmth. Thomas turned from the pond and started back towards home but stopped short when an older woman dropped her groceries nearby. As he helped her gather scattered fruits and vegetables, he listened—really listened—to her thanks laced with relief. In her eyes shone a gratitude that spoke volumes about dignity and kindness.

Walking away from her grateful smile, Thomas felt a shift within himself—a silent acknowledgment that perhaps this path toward greater emotional intelligence wasn't just about fixing tomorrow's meeting or mending team dynamics. Maybe it was about enriching every interaction with genuine understanding and empathy.

Could learning to pause like this be what leads us closer not just to others' hearts but also back to our own?

Unleashing Emotional Intelligence: Your Path to Personal Mastery

Emotional intelligence (EI) is often perceived as a static trait—something you're born with. However, the truth is far more empowering. EI is a skill that can be developed and honed through intentional practice and strategies. This chapter delves into the transformative process of enhancing emotional intelligence through practical, actionable steps that anyone can integrate into their daily lives.

The Power of Emotional Awareness

The journey to greater emotional intelligence begins with self-awareness. Here, we explore how tools like *journaling and mindful observation* serve as mirrors reflecting our emotional landscape. We gain insights into our emotional triggers and patterns by documenting our feelings and reactions. This increased awareness is the cornerstone of EI, as it allows us to navigate our feelings more effectively and respond rather than react in challenging situations.

The Art of Engagement and Listening

Listening isn't just about hearing words; it's about understanding the emotions behind them. We will discuss how *active listening* can transform relationships, fostering deeper connections and mutual respect. Additionally, seeking and interpreting *feedback* is critical for personal growth, providing external perspectives on our emotional responses that we might otherwise miss.

Empathy: Walking in Another's Shoes

Empathy extends beyond mere sympathy—it involves deeply understanding and sharing the feelings of others. This chapter highlights how developing empathy enhances our interpersonal relationships and enriches our inner emotional life, allowing for a more compassionate engagement with the world around us.

Mastering the Pause

One of the most potent tools in emotional regulation is learning to pause. This brief moment of stillness can distinguish between an impulsive reaction and a thoughtful response. The benefits of this practice are profound, affecting everything from personal relationships to professional interactions.

Through these strategies, you will discover that improving your emotional intelligence is possible and essential for achieving a harmonious life. Each step forward in this journey enhances your interactions with others and deepens your relationship with yourself.

By embracing these practices, you set a path toward better emotional understanding and a more fulfilled and resilient life. This chapter promises to be both a guide and a companion in your continuous journey of emotional growth.

Emotional intelligence is not a fixed trait but a skill that can be honed through practical exercises. *Increasing emotional awareness is the first step towards mastering emotional intelligence.* Journaling is a powerful tool that allows individuals to reflect on their emotions, thoughts, and reactions. By putting pen to paper, one can gain clarity on their feelings, identify patterns in their behavior, and track their emotional growth over time. Mindful observation is another effective practice that involves paying attention to one's emotions without judgment. By observing how emotions arise and manifest in different situations, individuals can better understand their inner workings.

Practicing these exercises regularly can lead to profound insights into one's emotional landscape. Journaling helps process complex emotions, resolve inner conflicts, and foster self-awareness. Mindful observation cultivates the ability to respond thoughtfully rather than impulsively to challenging situations. These practices lay the foundation for building emotional intelligence by encouraging individuals to engage with their emotions consciously and constructively.

Developing emotional awareness through journaling and mindful observation sets the stage for further growth in emotional intelligence. By becoming more attuned to their feelings and reactions, individuals can start making informed choices about expressing themselves and interacting with others. These exercises provide a solid framework for developing self-awareness for effective emotion regulation and interpersonal relationships.

Ready to delve deeper into practical strategies for enhancing your emotional intelligence? Read on to discover how feedback, active listening, empathy, and the art of pause can further elevate your emotional awareness and management skills.

Feedback, active listening, and empathy are three pillars that support the development of emotional intelligence. *Feedback* is a valuable tool for self-improvement, providing insights into our behaviors and their impact on others. By actively seeking feedback from trusted sources, we can better understand how our actions are perceived and make necessary adjustments to enhance our emotional intelligence. Constructive feedback mirrors our strengths and areas for growth, guiding us toward a more balanced and insightful approach to managing emotions.

Active listening is another essential skill in the pursuit of emotional intelligence. It involves not only hearing but truly understanding the message being conveyed by others. We demonstrate respect and empathy towards the speaker by actively engaging in conversations with an open mind and heart. Active listening allows us to connect deeper, fostering trust and mutual understanding. Through this practice, we can develop stronger relationships built on genuine communication and emotional awareness.

Empathy, the ability to understand and share the feelings of others, is a cornerstone of emotional intelligence. Cultivating empathy requires us to put ourselves in someone else's shoes, seeing the world from their perspective. By empathizing with others, we show compassion and kindness, strengthening interpersonal connections and fostering a sense of unity. Empathy enables us to respond to others with sensitivity and understanding, creating a supportive environment where emotions are acknowledged and validated.

In developing emotional intelligence, feedback guides us toward self-improvement, active listening acts as a bridge connecting us to others, and empathy illuminates the path toward deeper emotional connections. *Integrating these practices into daily interactions* can enhance our emotional intelligence and cultivate harmonious personal and professional relationships. These skills contribute to a more profound understanding of ourselves and those around us, increasing emotional awareness and effective emotion management.

Feedback, active listening, and empathy form a triad of essential tools for navigating the complexities of human emotions. They empower us to communicate more effectively, build stronger relationships, and navigate conflicts with grace and understanding. As we embrace these practices in our quest for emotional intelligence, we open ourselves to new possibilities for personal growth and fulfillment. By honing these skills with intention and dedication, we pave the way for a more harmonious life enriched by meaningful connections and authentic interactions.

Learning to pause is a powerful tool for effective emotion management. *In our fast-paced world, pausing and reflecting can significantly change how we respond to situations*. Pausing allows us to step back from our immediate emotions, giving us the space to contemplate our reactions. *By incorporating pausing into our daily lives, we can cultivate a sense of calm and clarity*.

Pausing is not about suppressing emotions but rather about acknowledging them. When we pause, we recognize what we are feeling without judgment. This practice helps us become more aware of our feelings and better understand their triggers. *Through this awareness, we can choose how to respond instead of reacting impulsively*.

One critical benefit of pausing is that it allows us to break the cycle of automatic reactions. When faced with challenging situations, our immediate response is often driven by habit or past experiences. *We interrupt this pattern by pausing and creating space for more intentional and mindful responses*. This can lead to better outcomes in our interactions and navigating various circumstances.

Pausing also allows us to regulate our emotions. When we take a moment before responding, we can assess the intensity of our feelings and decide on a suitable course of action. *This self-regulation is crucial for maintaining healthy relationships and managing conflicts effectively*. It empowers us to express ourselves constructively and considerately.

Moreover, pausing fosters emotional resilience. When faced with adversity or challenging emotions, pausing allows us to gather our thoughts and approach the situation comfortably. *This resilience enables us to bounce back from setbacks and navigate difficulties with grace and strength*.

Incorporating pauses into our daily interactions can also enhance our communication skills. By taking a moment before responding, we can genuinely listen to what others are saying and respond with empathy and understanding. *This active listening promotes deeper connections with those around us and fosters a sense of mutual respect.*

Learning *to pause is a valuable skill that supports emotional intelligence development.* Integrating pauses into our daily routines allows us to cultivate self-awareness, regulate our emotions effectively, build resilience, improve communication, and foster stronger relationships. *Pausing empowers us to navigate life's challenges with mindfulness and emotional maturity.*

Emotional intelligence is a skill that can be honed and refined through intentional practice and commitment. This chapter has explored several practical strategies that enhance emotional awareness and foster deeper relationships and personal growth. By integrating activities like *journaling* and *mindful observation* into daily routines, individuals can significantly heighten their understanding of their emotional landscapes.

Moreover, the role of *feedback, active listening, and empathy* in developing emotional intelligence cannot be overstated. These elements are crucial for building trust and understanding personally and professionally. Learning to pause, a simple yet powerful tool helps manage reactions and emotions more effectively, ensuring thoughtful responses rather than impulsive reactions.

Mastering Empathy through Active Listening

Developing empathy through active listening is a transformative journey that enhances interpersonal connections and emotional insight. Here's how you can implement this in your daily interactions:

1. *Focus on the Speaker*: Ensure full attention during conversations by eliminating distractions, maintaining eye contact, and adopting open body language.

1. *Practice Active Listening*: Engage with the speaker using nods, appropriate facial expressions, and verbal affirmations like "mm-hmm" to encourage them to share openly.

1. *Ask Clarifying Questions*: After they finish, clarify any doubts by asking questions that probe deeper into their thoughts and feelings without making assumptions.

1. *Reflect and Summarize*: Show that you've understood by paraphrasing key points. This reflection helps the speaker feel valued and heard.

Show Empathy: Respond with empathetic statements acknowledging their feelings, showing support and understanding.

1. *Provide Feedback*: If asked, offer thoughtful feedback based on your observations, delivered with respect and kindness.

1. *Practice Regularly*: Incorporate these steps into everyday conversations with different people to turn active listening into a habitual skill.

Implementing this process not only deepens understanding but also reinforces the emotional bonds that are essential for effective communication and relationship building.

BY COMMITTING TO THESE

practices, you are on your way to

mastering emotional intelligence, which will undoubtedly enrich your personal and professional endeavors. Remember, the journey to enhanced emotional intelligence is continuous, and each step taken is a step towards a more aware and connected existence. Embrace these strategies with openness and persistence, and watch as your world transforms through more explicit communication, stronger relationships, and heightened emotional awareness.

Chapter 5: Emotions in Action: Leveraging Feelings for Success

As the sun dipped below the horizon, casting a golden hue across the bustling city streets, Anna sat at a small, weathered table in the corner of her favorite café. The clatter of cups and murmurs of conversation surrounded her, a comforting cacophony that usually soothed her thoughts. Today, however, was different. She was grappling with a decision that felt heavier than usual—a potential career move that promised advancement but required relocating to a new city.

Anna sipped her coffee slowly, feeling its warmth as she pondered her options. Her mind wandered back to last week's meeting, where her boss had laid out the opportunities and challenges of the new position. It was an exciting prospect but one that demanded careful thought. The emotional weight of leaving behind friends and familiar settings battled with the logical benefits of professional growth.

A child's laughter broke through her reverie, pulling Anna's attention to a young family at the following table. The parents interacted with gentle smiles and understanding nods as their little one babbled about his day at school. Witnessing this simple exchange sparked Anna's realization of the importance of empathy—not just in personal relationships but also in fostering effective professional environments.

She recalled instances where understanding a colleague's perspective had led to better collaborative outcomes and how those moments were not just about solving problems but building relationships. The thought made it clear that cultivating empathy would be critical to her success wherever she decided to go.

TURNING BACK TO HER decision, Anna considered how she could leverage her emotional intelligence strategically in either scenario—staying or going. Staying meant deepening existing relationships and continuing projects she was passionate about; leaving meant new challenges and broadening her professional network.

The waiter brought over a fresh pot of coffee, interrupting Anna's thoughts momentarily as he poured with practiced ease. She thanked him with a smile, appreciating the brief interaction that grounded her back to the present moment.

As Anna stared out into the dimming light outside, thoughts swirling like leaves in a soft breeze, she wondered: How might embracing strategic emotional leverage influence my immediate decision and shape my approach to future challenges?

Harness the Power of Emotions for Unprecedented Success

Emotions are often seen as obstacles to clear thinking and effective decision-making. However, when properly harnessed and understood, emotions can be powerful tools that enhance our interactions, improve our self-perception, and ultimately lead to greater success in both personal and professional realms. This chapter delves into the strategic leverage of emotions, illustrating how a well-managed emotional state can influence rational decision-making and foster stronger relationships.

The Art of Emotional Decision-Making

The first key area we will explore is the *rational decision-making process influenced by well-managed emotions*. Contrary to popular belief that emotions cloud judgment, they can provide essential data about our values and priorities. Acknowledging and analyzing our feelings before making decisions can align our choices more closely with our authentic selves. This approach enhances personal integrity and increases the likelihood of achieving long-lasting satisfaction with our choices.

Enhancing Interactions Through Emotional Intelligence

Next, we will discuss how *strategic emotional leverage can enhance personal and professional interactions*. Emotions are integral to communication; they signal what matters to us and can help persuade or dissuade others. When we express our emotions effectively, it opens up new avenues for collaboration and innovation. Understanding the emotional dynamics at play in professional settings can lead to better teamwork, leadership, and customer relationships.

Empathy: The Bridge to Meaningful Connections

Finally, we will analyze *the **role of empathy in fostering more robust, meaningful relationships*** and community ties. Empathy allows us to see the world from another's perspective and share their feelings. It is a critical skill in building networks of support, resolving conflicts, and nurturing deep connections. Enhancing our empathetic abilities opens us to richer human experiences and a more compassionate society.

This chapter provides practical advice on developing these skills through real-life examples, expert opinions, and actionable tips. Each section is designed to inform and transform your approach to emotional intelligence—turning it from a concept into a tangible tool for success.

Through this exploration, it becomes evident *that **emotional intelligence is about controlling or understanding one's emotions and maneuvering through social landscapes with agility and purpose***. Mastering this art can lead to more fulfilling and successful interactions, whether in boardrooms or living rooms.

THIS NARRATIVE AIMS not only at intellectual understanding but also at creating a blueprint for action—encouraging you to experiment with these techniques daily. By embracing your emotions as allies rather than adversaries, you unlock a new dimension of personal empowerment and social effectiveness that can profoundly impact your journey toward harmony and success.

Emotions play a significant role in our decision-making process, often influencing the outcomes of our choices. When we effectively manage our feelings, we are better equipped to make rational decisions that serve our best interests. A well-managed emotional state allows us to approach situations with clarity and objectivity, enabling us to consider various factors before deciding. Understanding our emotions and their impact on our thought processes will allow us to navigate complex scenarios more quickly and confidently.

Self-awareness is vital in managing emotions for rational decision-making. Recognizing our emotional triggers and understanding how they affect our judgment empowers us to respond thoughtfully rather than impulsively. Taking the time to assess our emotional state before making decisions allows us to consider the situation from a balanced perspective, considering our feelings and logical reasoning.

Emotional regulation is another crucial aspect of making rational decisions influenced by emotions. By regulating our emotions effectively, we can prevent overwhelming feelings from clouding judgment. This involves techniques such as deep breathing, mindfulness, or reframing negative thoughts to maintain calm when faced with challenging choices.

Empathy also plays a significant role in decision-making influenced by emotions. Understanding the feelings of others involved in a situation can provide valuable insights that help us make more informed decisions. By empathizing with different perspectives and considering how others may feel, we can approach decision-making with compassion and fairness, leading to outcomes that benefit all parties involved.

Incorporating emotional *intelligence* into our decision-making process enhances our ability to navigate complex emotions effectively. By developing self-awareness, emotional regulation, and empathy skills, we can make decisions that are rational and considerate of the emotional landscape surrounding the situation.

This holistic approach to decision-making enables us to leverage emotions as valuable tools in achieving personal and professional success.

Continue reading about how strategic emotional leverage can enhance personal and professional interactions.

Emotions play a crucial role in shaping our personal and professional interactions. When managed strategically, emotions can enhance relationships and propel us towards success. By understanding the power of emotions and learning to harness them effectively, we can navigate social dynamics with finesse and authenticity.

Emotional intelligence allows us to connect on a deeper level with others in personal relationships. When we are attuned to our emotions and those of the people around us, we can respond empathetically and build stronger bonds. We create a positive environment that fosters trust and mutual understanding by expressing genuine interest and care for others' feelings.

Emotional leverage can be a powerful tool for communication and collaboration in professional settings. Awareness of our emotions enables us to navigate conflicts constructively and communicate our needs effectively. By managing emotions such as frustration or stress, we can maintain a professional demeanor and make rational decisions that benefit us and our colleagues.

Empathy plays a significant role in enhancing personal and professional interactions. When we put ourselves in someone else's shoes and strive to understand their perspective, we cultivate empathy. This ability to empathize allows us to forge meaningful connections, resolve conflicts peacefully, and collaborate more productively toward shared goals.

By strategically leveraging emotions, we can create a harmonious balance between rational decision-making and emotional intelligence. Emotions provide valuable insights into our own needs and the needs of others, guiding us towards more authentic and fulfilling interactions. When we approach every interaction with intentionality and emotional awareness, we pave the way for success in our personal relationships and professional endeavors.

Ultimately, by mastering the art of emotional leverage, we empower ourselves to navigate the complexities of human interactions with grace and wisdom. Embracing our emotions not as obstacles but as valuable guides open up new possibilities for growth, connection, and achievement. Through strategic emotional management, we can cultivate more prosperous relationships, foster empathy, and enhance our overall well-being in all aspects of life.

Emotional Leverage Process Model

The Emotional Leverage Process Model is a structured framework designed to help individuals effectively utilize their emotions to enhance decision-making and interpersonal interactions. It consists of five key stages that guide individuals through recognizing, analyzing, strategizing, executing, and reflecting on their emotions deliberately and intentionally. Each stage is crucial in empowering individuals to leverage their emotions as tools for personal and professional success.

Recognition

The first stage of the Emotional Leverage Process Model is ***Recognition***. In this phase, individuals are encouraged to accurately identify and name their emotions. This step is essential as it lays the foundation for understanding one's emotional state before proceeding. Individuals can understand how their emotions may influence their thoughts and behaviors by acknowledging their feelings.

Analysis

The following recognition comes to the *Analysis stage*. Here, individuals delve deeper into why a particular emotion has surfaced and how it might impact their actions. By examining the root cause of their feelings and considering the potential consequences of acting upon them, individuals can make more informed decisions about how to proceed. This stage encourages introspection and self-awareness, enabling individuals to navigate their emotions effectively.

Strategy

The *Strategy* stage involves planning how to utilize the identified emotion positively. Individuals consider how to leverage their emotions to motivate themselves, communicate more effectively with others, or gain a new perspective. This phase is about harnessing emotional energy constructively aligning with personal goals and values.

Execution

Once a strategy has been formulated, individuals move into the *Execution* phase. They put their plan into action by incorporating their emotions into decision-making processes or interactions with others. By consciously using their emotions as tools rather than being controlled by them, individuals can enhance the quality of their responses and achieve more favorable outcomes.

Reflection

The final stage of the Emotional Leverage Process Model is *Reflection*. After executing their strategy, individuals evaluate the results of incorporating emotions into their actions. This reflective practice allows for learning from experiences, understanding the impact of emotional leverage on outcomes, and refining strategies for future use. Reflection fosters continuous growth and improvement in emotional intelligence.

In summary, the *Emotional Leverage Process Model* provides a systematic approach to harnessing emotions effectively. By progressing through the stages of *Recognition, Analysis, Strategy, Execution, and Reflection*, individuals can develop greater self-awareness, make informed decisions based on emotional insights, and cultivate stronger interpersonal relationships in both personal and professional spheres.

Emotions, often perceived as obstacles to rational thinking, can be powerful allies when understood and managed effectively. Throughout this chapter, we've explored how a well-managed emotional state forms the bedrock of rational decision-making. By integrating emotions into our decision-making process, we enhance our personal and professional interactions and deepen our understanding of ourselves and others.

Strategic emotional leverage is not just about controlling emotions but also using them to navigate complex social landscapes. By recognizing the emotional currents within ourselves and others, we can tailor our interactions to be more effective and harmonious. This approach transforms potential conflicts into opportunities for collaboration and mutual understanding.

Empathy plays a pivotal role in this dynamic. It allows us to connect with others on a deeper level, fostering meaningful and enduring relationships. The ability to empathize does not merely improve our personal lives; it also has profound implications for community building and professional environments. Empathy can create a more inclusive and supportive atmosphere where individuals feel understood and valued.

The skills and insights discussed here are essential for anyone looking to thrive personally and professionally. By embracing and applying these principles, you can achieve a more balanced and fulfilling life. Remember, emotional intelligence is not an innate talent but a set of skills that can be learned and honed. Each step you take to understand and manage your emotions is a step towards a more harmonious and prosperous future.

Embrace the journey of emotional mastery with patience and persistence. As we have seen, the rewards extend far beyond simple personal gain—they enrich every aspect of our lives, creating ripples that impact our communities and workplaces. Let us continue to learn, grow,

and leverage our emotions for success and a deeper connection with the
world around us.

Chapter 6: The Truth About Emotional Agility: Dispelling the Myths

Thomas walked briskly to his office in the chilled morning air of a bustling city. The crunch of autumn leaves underfoot mingled with the distant hum of traffic, painting a symphony of routine. Today, however, his mind wrestled with an intricate dilemma that disrupted this familiar tune.

Thomas was the director of a nonprofit focused on youth education and development. Recently, he faced a critical decision about funding that threatened to splinter his team. The choice was between continuing support for an effective but costly program that served fewer children or shifting funds to a broader, less intensive program that could reach more but with potentially less impact per child.

As he entered the office, the sharp scent of coffee wafted from the break room, pulling him momentarily from his thoughts. He greeted his colleagues with a nod and a smile — his usual mask of composure, barely hiding the turmoil underneath.

Sitting at his desk, Thomas gazed out the window at the city below. He thought about emotional intelligence and its misconceptions. It wasn't just about being agreeable or making decisions that everyone liked; it was about navigating through emotions to make choices that, while challenging, were necessary for the greater good. His role demanded empathy and courage to face potential backlash for unpopular decisions.

The phone rang, snapping him back to reality. Clara from Human Resources wanted to discuss her concerns about the potential impacts of funding changes on staff morale and workload. As they spoke, Thomas listened intently, weighing each word against his apprehensions and hopes for the organization's mission.

After hanging up, he leaned back in his chair and sighed deeply.

The room felt suddenly quiet around him — as if waiting for a verdict.

Was he ready to make a decision that could redefine their work but possibly alienate some of his team? Could he manage the emotional fallout while steering them toward what he believed was a more sustainable path?

Unveiling the Real Faces of Emotional Intelligence

Emotional Intelligence (EI) is frequently misunderstood as being agreeable and non-confrontational. However, accurate emotional intelligence goes much deeper, involving a nuanced approach to managing emotions to foster authentic and robust relationships. In this chapter, we will debunk common myths surrounding EI, emphasizing that it is not about pleasing everyone but about making wise, sometimes tough decisions that uphold the health of relationships and lead to successful personal and collective outcomes.

EI is often mistaken for mere agreeableness, leading to avoidance of necessary confrontations and a lack of genuine interaction. This misconception undermines emotional intelligence's core benefits, enabling individuals to navigate complex social landscapes with clarity and purpose. We aim to provide a clearer picture of what EI involves by addressing these misconceptions.

The Importance of Authenticity

The ability to express emotions authentically is central to effective relationship management. Authenticity requires balance—it is not about unfiltered expression of every emotion but about understanding and communicating feelings in a respectful and considerate way. This chapter will explore how balanced emotional expressions are crucial to healthy interpersonal dynamics.

Navigating Tough Decisions with EI

Another facet of emotional intelligence involves making decisions that may not be popular but are necessary for relationships' greater good or long-term sustainability. These scenarios often require a firm grasp of EI to navigate successfully. We will delve into examples where emotionally intelligent responses have paved the way for better outcomes despite initial resistance or displeasure from others.

Throughout this discussion, we will focus on real-life applications of these principles. By integrating stories of individuals who have successfully applied EI in challenging situations, we aim to illustrate the tangible benefits and transformative potential of mastering emotional intelligence.

Our exploration will clarify what emotional intelligence truly entails and equip you with the knowledge to apply these insights in your life. The goal is to foster an environment where you can thrive personally and professionally by making informed, emotionally intelligent decisions.

This chapter demystifies emotional intelligence and corrects widespread misconceptions. It sets the stage for a deeper understanding and practical application of EI principles in daily interactions and decision-making processes. Embrace the journey towards becoming more emotionally intelligent to improve your relationships and enhance your overall quality of life.

Emotional intelligence is often misunderstood, with one of the most common misconceptions being that individuals high in emotional intelligence are overly agreeable. While being emotionally intelligent does involve understanding others' emotions and empathizing with them, it does not mean constantly striving to please everyone at the expense of personal authenticity. *Emotional intelligence is about navigating emotions effectively, both in oneself and in others, to build genuine and strong relationships.*

This may involve making tough decisions or setting boundaries that are not always pleasing to everyone but are essential for maintaining healthy relationships and achieving personal or collective goals.

Agreeableness is just one facet of emotional intelligence.

Accurate emotional intelligence encompasses a range of skills, including self-awareness, self-regulation, empathy, and social skills. It's about being attuned to one's emotions and the emotions of others, managing them appropriately, and using this awareness to guide behavior effectively. ***It's not about avoiding conflict or discomfort at all costs but about handling them constructively.***

In many situations, prioritizing agreeableness over authenticity can lead to superficial relationships and personal dissatisfaction. ***Being authentic in our emotional expressions can foster genuine connections based on mutual respect and understanding.*** It allows for open communication and resolving conflicts healthily rather than burying emotions to maintain a facade of agreeableness.

Striking a balance between agreeableness and authenticity is crucial for building meaningful relationships. It involves expressing emotions honestly while also considering the feelings of others. This nuanced approach can lead to more profound connections based on trust and mutual support rather than mere pleasantries that lack depth.

Keep reading to discover how managing emotions authentically can transform your relationships and empower you in decision-making situations.

In navigating relationships, ***authentic and balanced emotional expressions*** play a pivotal role. Genuine emotional responses help build trust and connection with others, fostering a sense of understanding and empathy. When individuals express their emotions sincerely, it creates an environment where openness and vulnerability are valued, leading to more profound relationships.

Balanced emotional expressions involve acknowledging and managing one's feelings effectively without suppressing or exaggerating them.

Authenticity in emotional expressions allows individuals to communicate their true thoughts and feelings, promoting relationship transparency. When people express themselves genuinely, it fosters an atmosphere of honesty and integrity, laying the foundation for meaningful connections. Being authentic in one's emotions also enables others to reciprocate with their genuine feelings, leading to mutual understanding and rapport.

Balanced emotional expressions involve regulating emotions appropriately in various situations to maintain harmony and respect in relationships. It is essential to find a middle ground between underreacting and overreacting emotionally. By striking this balance, individuals can navigate conversations and interactions smoothly, fostering healthy communication and mutual respect.

In relationship management, *authentic emotional expressions* serve as a bridge for genuine connection with others. When individuals express their emotions sincerely and openly, it cultivates trust and strengthens their bond. Authenticity fosters a safe space for both parties to share their feelings honestly, leading to deeper understanding and empathy in the relationship.

Moreover, *balanced emotional expressions contribute* to effective conflict resolution and problem-solving within relationships. By managing emotions appropriately, individuals can address conflicts rationally and constructively without letting heightened emotions escalate the situation. This ability to regulate emotions paves the way for productive discussions and collaborative solutions that strengthen the relationship.

In summary, *authenticity* and *balance* in emotional expressions are crucial aspects of relationship management. Individuals can foster trust, build stronger connections, resolve conflicts effectively, and cultivate harmonious relationships based on mutual respect and understanding by being genuine in expressing emotions and maintaining a balanced approach to emotional regulation.

In navigating the realm of emotional intelligence, there are instances where tough decisions must be made, even if they are unpopular. *Emotional intelligence often requires individuals to prioritize long-term goals and healthy relationships over short-term gratification or popularity.* These scenarios can be challenging but crucial for personal growth and authentic connections. *By embodying emotional intelligence, individuals can make decisions that may not please everyone but align with their values and objectives.*

One key aspect of emotional intelligence is the ability to make difficult decisions in adversity. This may involve setting boundaries, delivering constructive criticism, or making choices that challenge the status quo. *While these decisions may not always be well-received by others, they are essential for personal development and fostering genuine relationships. Emotional intelligence empowers individuals to stay true to themselves while navigating complex social dynamics.*

In some situations, emotional intelligence demands tough choices that require courage and resilience. This could mean addressing conflicts head-on, standing up for what is right, or taking risks for personal or collective growth. *By embracing these challenges with emotional agility, individuals can cultivate stronger relationships built on trust and authenticity. These decisions may not always be easy, but they are vital for personal integrity and growth.*

Emotional intelligence also involves understanding that not every decision will be met with immediate approval or praise. It requires the willingness to prioritize authenticity and honesty over seeking constant validation from others. *By staying true to one's values and principles, individuals can establish trust and respect in their relationships*, even if it means making unpopular choices.

Ultimately, emotional intelligence equips individuals with the tools to navigate difficult situations with grace and composure. It enables them to make decisions based on empathy, self-awareness, and a deep understanding of their emotions and those of others. *By embracing the discomfort of tough decision-making with emotional agility*, individuals can pave the way for personal growth, stronger relationships, and a more fulfilling life journey.

Throughout this chapter, we've unraveled some common misconceptions about emotional intelligence (EI), highlighting its true essence beyond mere agreeableness. It's crucial to understand that EI isn't always about saying 'yes' or pleasing everyone. Instead, it's about managing our emotions effectively to build stronger, more authentic relationships and making decisions that, while sometimes tough, are necessary for long-term benefits.

Emotional intelligence demands a balance between genuine expression and thoughtful interaction. This balance ensures that our relationships are both sincere and strategically sound. By fostering this understanding, we empower ourselves to handle interpersonal dynamics skillfully, enhancing personal and professional connections.

Moreover, the scenarios discussed exemplify that EI often requires us to make difficult choices. These decisions might only sometimes be popular, but they are crucial for maintaining the health and integrity of our relationships and achieving our overarching goals.

The ability to navigate these complex situations with emotional savvy marks high emotional intelligence.

Embracing the full spectrum of emotional intelligence involves recognizing its role in fostering resilience and inspiring personal growth. As we become more adept at using our emotional insights effectively, we improve our lives and influence those around us positively.

By integrating the insights from this chapter, you are better equipped to approach emotional intelligence with a clear, nuanced understanding. This knowledge is theoretical and immensely practical, paving the way for enhanced relationships and greater success in various facets of life. Remember, the journey to mastering EI is continuous, and each step forward is a step towards a more harmonious life.

Chapter 7: IQ vs. EI: Tapping into Emotional Versus Intellectual Strengths

The early morning sun shone gently through the high windows of the university library, where Thomas sat surrounded by stacks of books on psychology and human behavior. His mind was a battleground of thoughts as he sifted through theories and research papers, each page turning like a clock ticking in his quest for understanding. He was searching for the delicate balance between emotional intelligence (EI) and intellectual intelligence (IQ), trying to grasp how each contributed to personal development and societal interaction.

Outside, the world hurried by; students rushed to their classes, their laughter and chatter floating through the open window, momentarily pulling Thomas from his reverie. He watched them for a moment, pondering how each interaction was influenced by unseen forces of logic and emotion. His gaze returned to an article discussing a study where EI had significantly predicted leadership success over IQ, highlighting that understanding emotions could be as critical as analytical skills in professional environments.

Thomas rubbed his temples, feeling the weight of his upcoming thesis defense. He had chosen to explore how nurturing both types of intelligence could lead to more balanced personal and professional lives. The stakes were high; his future career as a psychologist depended on convincing his professors that these dual aspects of intelligence were not just academically exciting but essential life skills.

He recalled last week's heated debate with Professor Jenkins, who had argued that intellectual pursuits often overshadowed emotional development in academic settings. Thomas had countered with anecdotes from his own life, explaining how his failures and successes seemed equally tied to his ability to manage emotions and solve problems.

As he looked around the quiet library filled with earnest learners, Thomas wondered if they recognized this balance within themselves. Did they see their studies as merely steps toward degrees and careers or as part of a broader journey toward understanding themselves and others?

A cool breeze fluttered some papers off the table, snapping him back from these musings. He gathered them, each sheet whispering questions about human nature and societal constructs. How much did our emotional aptitude really weigh against our intellectual prowess? And how did one cultivate an environment that valued both? These questions lingered in the air like the faint scent of old books surrounding him—essential yet elusive elements in the vast expanse of human understanding.

Unveiling the Dual Dynamics of Intelligence: A Path to Personal Mastery

When we speak of intelligence, the general inclination is to think about academic prowess or logical reasoning. However, a profound component often overlooked is Emotional Intelligence (EI), which plays an equally crucial role in our lives. In this exploration, we explore how EI and Intellectual Intelligence (IQ) serve distinct yet interconnected functions in shaping our personal development and social interactions.

Understanding the dichotomy between EI and IQ is fundamental to grasping their impact on our lives. IQ typically measures our ability to analyze, reason, and apply logic. These capabilities are often quantified through standardized tests and are seen as predictors of academic and professional success. On the other hand, EI involves our ability to manage our own emotions and those of others, fostering empathy, conflict resolution skills, and deeper interpersonal relationships.

The interaction between these two forms of intelligence significantly influences how we navigate the world. For instance, while a high IQ can land someone a top job, their EI often determines how well they manage their role and relate with colleagues. This chapter aims to further dissect these roles, emphasizing that *both types of intelligence are essential for a successful life*—professionally and personally.

We will explore *how both EI and IQ contribute uniquely to societal interactions*. While IQ might dominate in settings requiring quick problem-solving or critical thinking, EI steers team dynamics and leadership. The importance lies in possessing these skills and balancing them depending on the context.

Moreover, nurturing both dimensions of intelligence can lead to more balanced personal interactions and professional environments. High-IQ individuals may excel in data-driven environments but struggle in leadership roles if their EI needs to be developed. Conversely, those with high EI might excel in social settings but face challenges in technical roles requiring strong analytical skills.

This discussion will also cover practical insights on *enhancing emotional and intellectual capacities*. Just as there are methods to improve cognitive functions, such as memory and analytical skills, there are proven strategies to enhance one's emotional understanding and regulation. Recognizing that these capabilities are not fixed but can be developed is empowering.

This chapter sets the stage for a deeper understanding of how integrating intellectual rigor with emotional depth can lead to more fulfilling personal relationships and effective professional interactions. By nurturing both aspects of intelligence, individuals can achieve a more harmonious balance in life, underscoring the importance of a holistic approach to personal development.

This chapter invites you to reflect on your own experiences with IQ and EI and encourages an introspective look at how you might cultivate these skills further to enhance your personal growth and your interactions within society.

Emotional Intelligence (EI) and Intellectual Intelligence (IQ) are two distinct but equally important aspects of human intelligence. While IQ focuses on cognitive abilities like problem-solving and critical thinking, EI involves understanding and managing emotions effectively. ***Both types of intelligence play crucial roles in personal development***, but they operate in different spheres of life.

Intellectual Intelligence (IQ) is often associated with academic success and cognitive abilities. It involves logical reasoning, problem-solving skills, memory capacity, and analytical thinking. Individuals with high IQs excel in tasks that require strategic planning, mathematical calculations, and abstract reasoning. ***IQ is essential for academic achievements, professional success in specific fields***, and tasks that demand logical reasoning and intellectual prowess.

However, emotional Intelligence (EI) deals with recognizing, understanding, and managing emotions effectively. It encompasses empathy, self-awareness, social skills, emotional regulation, and interpersonal relationships. People with high EI can navigate social situations adeptly, manage conflicts peacefully, and build strong connections with others. ***EI is crucial for building healthy relationships***, resolving disputes amicably, and maintaining emotional well-being.

Balancing both types of intelligence is vital to well-rounded personal development. While IQ helps in academic or professional settings that require analytical thinking and problem-solving skills, EI is essential for emotional well-being and successful interpersonal relationships. Striking a balance between the two can lead to holistic growth and overall life satisfaction.

Understanding the differences between IQ and EI can help individuals identify their strengths and areas for improvement. ***By*** *honing both types of intelligence,* individuals can achieve success not only in their careers but also in their personal lives.

Recognizing the value of emotional intelligence alongside intellectual intelligence can lead to more fulfilling relationships, better communication skills, and improved overall well-being.

Continue reading to explore how both EI and IQ contribute to distinct aspects of societal interactions and professional success.

Both *emotional intelligence (EI) and intellectual intelligence (IQ)* play crucial roles in our lives, especially in societal interactions and professional success. *Emotional intelligence* enables individuals to navigate complex social situations with empathy, understanding, and self-awareness. It involves recognizing and managing emotions in oneself and others, fostering better relationships and effective communication. On the other hand, *intellectual intelligence* encompasses cognitive abilities such as problem-solving, critical thinking, and logical reasoning, which are essential for academic and professional success.

Emotional intelligence shines through in societal interactions in the way individuals handle conflicts, show empathy toward others, and build meaningful connections. Those with high EI can diffuse tense situations, understand different perspectives, and collaborate effectively in group settings. Conversely, *intellectual intelligence* aids in analytical thinking, strategic planning, and decision-making processes often required in complex social structures.

When it comes to *professional success*, both EI and IQ are valuable assets. *Emotional intelligence* is crucial in leadership roles where managing teams, resolving conflicts, and inspiring others are essential skills. Leaders with high EI can create a positive work environment, boost employee morale, and drive organizational success through effective communication and relationship-building. On the other hand, *intellectual intelligence* is vital for technical roles that require problem-solving skills, innovation, and expertise in specific domains.

In today's fast-paced world, where collaboration and adaptability are crucial to success, ***emotional and intellectual intelligence*** balance is increasingly important. Individuals who excel in both areas can leverage their cognitive abilities to solve complex problems while fostering positive relationships with colleagues and clients. By simultaneously honing both types of intelligence, individuals can thrive in diverse professional environments and lead fulfilling personal lives marked by meaningful connections and achievements.

Integrated Intelligence Framework

The ***Integrated Intelligence Framework*** introduces a symbiotic relationship between emotional intelligence (EI) and intellectual intelligence (IQ). This model visualizes EI and IQ as two overlapping circles in a Venn diagram, highlighting areas where they complement each other. For instance, problem-solving requires logical reasoning from IQ and understanding the emotional impacts of EI. By integrating these two types of intelligence, individuals can enhance their leadership skills, conflict resolution abilities, and creativity.

Component 1: Reflective Practice for Bridging Cognitive and Emotional Perspectives

Role: This component focuses on the importance of self-reflection to bridge cognitive and emotional perspectives. By engaging in reflective practice, individuals can better understand how their thoughts and emotions influence their decision-making processes.

Characteristics: Reflective practice involves introspection, mindfulness, and critical analysis of thoughts and feelings. It encourages individuals to consider how their emotions affect their cognitive functions and vice versa.

Contribution: By bridging cognitive and emotional perspectives through reflective practice, individuals can make more balanced decisions considering rationality and emotional intelligence. This leads to improved problem-solving skills and enhanced interpersonal relationships.

Component 2: Cultivating Empathy Alongside Analytical Skills

Role: This component emphasizes the importance of empathy in conjunction with analytical skills. Empathy allows individuals to understand others' emotions, leading to better communication and relationship-building.

Characteristics: Cultivating empathy involves active listening, perspective-taking, and emotional attunement to others' feelings. It requires individuals to step into someone else's shoes to comprehend their emotional state.

Contribution: Combining empathy with analytical skills can help individuals navigate social interactions more effectively. Understanding others' emotions fosters trust and rapport and enables better conflict resolution, negotiation, and leadership capabilities.

Dynamics of the Model

The Integrated Intelligence Framework operates on the premise that EI and IQ are not isolated but interconnected elements crucial for personal development. Individuals cultivate emotional and intellectual intelligence simultaneously, creating a harmonious balance that enhances decision-making processes, interpersonal relationships, and overall well-being. The model functions best when individuals actively engage in practices that promote self-awareness, empathy, critical thinking, and emotional regulation.

Practical Implications

Practically applying the *Integrated Intelligence Framework* can improve leadership qualities, enhance conflict resolution strategies, and increase creativity in problem-solving scenarios. By leveraging emotional and intellectual intelligence in tandem, individuals can navigate professional challenges with greater resilience and effectiveness. Employing reflective practices alongside empathy-building techniques can transform how individuals approach decision-making processes and interpersonal dynamics.

The ***Integrated Intelligence Framework*** offers a structured approach to developing a balanced blend of emotional intelligence (EI) and intellectual intelligence (IQ). By recognizing the synergistic relationship between these two forms of intelligence and actively cultivating skills that bridge cognitive and emotional perspectives, individuals can unlock their full potential for personal growth and professional success.

In exploring the intricate relationship between emotional intelligence (EI) and intellectual intelligence (IQ), we've unveiled their distinct yet complementary roles in shaping our personal and professional lives. Both types of intelligence are indispensable, each contributing uniquely to navigating social environments and achieving success.

Emotional intelligence equips us to understand and manage our emotions and those of others. This capacity is fundamental in fostering strong relationships, resolving conflicts, and enhancing leadership qualities. It's about more than just feeling; it's about applying empathy and emotional awareness to every interaction. On the other hand, ***intellectual intelligence* involves** cognitive processes like reasoning, problem-solving, and learning. High IQ can lead to academic and professional achievements. Still, without EI, there might be a struggle in teamwork and interpersonal relationships.

The synergy between EI and IQ cannot be overstated. While each has its strengths, they are most effective when developed concurrently. Cultivating a balance between emotional savvy and intellectual acumen offers a more rounded approach to life's challenges. It enables better decision-making, improves communication skills, and builds resilience.

It's essential to recognize that nurturing both types of intelligence enhances individual capabilities and enriches interactions within our communities and workplaces. This understanding should empower us to invest equally in our emotional and intellectual growth.

As we continue on our journey of personal development, let's strive to strengthen our emotional and intellectual faculties. By doing so, we lay a robust foundation for a fulfilling and harmonious life characterized by improved relationships and career success. Embrace the journey of growing in both dimensions, as this balanced approach will lead to a more comprehensive understanding of oneself and the world.

Chapter 8: The Ongoing Journey: Embracing Continuous Emotional Learning

Sarah leaned against the cool, speckled granite of the kitchen counter, her eyes tracing the steam rising from her morning coffee like tendrils of thought trying to escape into the clear air. The clock ticked a soft, rhythmic beat that mimed her heartbeat — slow, steady, and filled with anticipation. Today was not just another day; it was the day she would meet with Tom after their last heated argument about their project deadlines. The anticipation of this meeting filled her with a mix of nerves and determination.

The memory of their last conversation played in her mind. Voices raised slightly more than usual, words carrying a sharpness neither had intended. She remembered how Tom's face had tightened, eyes narrowing not in anger but in frustration. She knew then that her own emotional reactions had mirrored his—a dance of expressions governed by misunderstood intentions.

As she sipped her coffee, Sarah allowed herself to sink into the chair, feeling its sturdy back support her like an old friend. Her mind wandered to what she had read last night about emotional intelligence: the continuous journey, the unending path of learning and adapting one's emotions and responses according to each unique situation. She realized this wasn't just about any skill that could be mastered overnight but a lifelong commitment, a journey that empowers and inspires.

She pondered on strategies to apply these insights today with Tom. She could start by acknowledging their previous missteps without placing blame, offering an olive branch through understanding rather than defensiveness. This could open a gateway for more honest and empathetic communication.

The room was filled with soft morning light filtering through the blinds, casting lines across the wooden floor that pointed toward resolution and growth. Sarah felt a gentle resolve build within her as she carefully planned her words in her mind.

Outside, a bird chirped persistently as if cheering her on from its perch on the window ledge. It struck Sarah then how everyday interactions were not just rehearsals, but the main stage for more significant roles in life's grand plays — each small exchange crafting more robust characters forged by emotional wisdom.

Wouldn't it be something if each conversation were seen as an opportunity to weave understanding and connection into our life's tapestry?

Is Your Emotional Intelligence Journey Ever Really Complete?

Emotional intelligence (EI) is not a destination but a continuous journey rich with opportunities for personal growth and improvement. As we delve deeper into understanding and managing our emotions, it becomes evident that each day offers a new landscape for applying these insights. This ongoing process is about learning to react and evolving proactively with each experience we encounter.

Emotional intelligence, as we've explored throughout this book, is foundational to fostering better relationships and achieving professional success. However, the mastery of EI is not achieved through static learning; instead, it requires a persistent commitment to self-reflection and adaptation. Every social interaction serves as a mini-classroom where emotional awareness, regulation, and management lessons can be practiced and perfected.

Lifelong Learning Through Emotional Interactions

One of the core elements of enhancing EI is recognizing its dynamic nature. The development of emotional intelligence doesn't stop when you feel you've achieved a certain level of mastery. There are always higher levels to reach and deeper insights to gain. This chapter reinforces the importance of seeing every interaction as a stepping stone in your EI journey. Whether a brief exchange with a coworker or a deep conversation with a loved one, each moment is an opportunity to apply and refine your emotional skills.

Strategies for Daily Emotional Excellence

Incorporating EI effectively into daily life requires practical strategies that can be seamlessly integrated into regular interactions. This chapter will explore how you can take the theoretical knowledge of EI and turn it into practical action. For instance, maintaining emotional balance during stressful situations could involve deep breathing exercises or reframing the situation positively. Enhancing empathy in relationships could be achieved by actively listening and validating the other person's feelings. The focus will be on actionable techniques that can be implemented immediately for noticeable improvements in both personal and professional realms.

Stories of Resilience and Adaptation

To inspire your commitment to this continuous journey, we will share personal stories highlighting the ongoing nature of EI development. These narratives will demonstrate how others have successfully navigated their emotional landscapes and how they've adapted their approach based on their experiences. By understanding their challenges and triumphs, you'll see how constant observation and adjustment are integral to mastering emotional intelligence.

Combining lifelong learning with everyday practice forms the cornerstone of truly mastering emotional intelligence. As we prepare to conclude our exploration in this book, remember that each chapter builds upon the last, aiming to equip you with a comprehensive understanding of EI. The ultimate goal has been to provide you with the tools necessary not just to understand and manage your emotions but also to positively influence those around you, thereby enhancing your relationships and professional success.

By embracing this journey, you embrace a life where emotions are not obstacles but instruments for achieving greater harmony and effectiveness in all areas of life. Let this chapter be both a capstone and a compass, guiding you toward continued growth and adaptation in your emotional intelligence voyage. Remember, the benefits of emotional intelligence are vast, from improved relationships to enhanced professional success. Keep these in mind as you navigate your journey.

Continuous emotional intelligence development unfolds gradually, offering numerous learning opportunities along the way. Just like any skill that improves with practice, emotional intelligence requires ongoing effort and dedication to cultivate. Each personal or professional interaction presents a chance to apply and refine emotional intelligence skills. *Enhancing emotional intelligence is not a one-time event but a continuous evolution that demands consistent engagement and reflection*

.

By recognizing that emotional intelligence is a lifelong pursuit, individuals can embrace each day as an opportunity to learn more about themselves and others. *Every interaction is a classroom where emotions are the textbooks, providing valuable insights into human behavior and relationships.* This understanding of emotional intelligence as a skill that can be honed over time empowers individuals to navigate life's complexities more easily.

Embracing the continuous nature of emotional intelligence development fosters personal growth and deepens self-awareness.

Through ongoing practice and reflection, individuals can refine their ability to recognize and regulate emotions effectively. Each experience offers a chance to learn more about emotional responses, communication styles, and interpersonal dynamics, contributing to enhanced relationships and well-being.

As individuals engage in the ongoing journey of mastering emotional intelligence, they become more attuned to their emotions and those of others. *This heightened awareness allows for more meaningful connections, improved conflict resolution skills, and enhanced empathy towards others' experiences.* By embracing the continuous development of emotional intelligence, individuals open themselves to a world of possibilities where personal growth and enriched relationships become the norm.

Continue reading for practical strategies on applying emotional intelligence insights in daily interactions and long-term relationships.

Applying Emotional Intelligence Insights in *Daily Interactions and Long-Term Relationships*

Strategies for Everyday Application

When it comes to incorporating emotional intelligence (EI) insights into our daily interactions and long-term relationships, consistency is key. *Consistent practice* allows us to hone our skills and genuinely embody the principles of EI in our interactions with others. One effective strategy is to *pause before reacting* to challenging situations. This moment of reflection gives us the space to consider our emotions and choose a response that aligns with our values and goals.

Active Listening and Empathy

Another crucial strategy is *active listening*. We show respect and empathy by genuinely listening to others without judgment or interruption. *Empathy* forms the foundation of solid relationships, allowing us to connect more deeply with those around us. When we practice active listening, we understand others better and cultivate a sense of trust and openness in our relationships.

Self-Awareness and Self-Regulation

Developing *self-awareness* is fundamental to applying EI insights effectively. Understanding our emotions, triggers, and biases allows us to navigate interactions with greater clarity and composure. *Self-regulation* closely follows self-awareness, enabling us to manage our emotional responses constructively.

Through self-regulation, we can avoid unnecessary conflicts and maintain harmonious relationships.

Conflict Resolution Techniques

Conflict is inevitable in long-term relationships. However, how we approach and resolve conflicts can significantly improve the quality of our relationships. *Conflict resolution techniques* grounded in EI principles can help us constructively navigate disagreements. By focusing on finding mutually beneficial solutions rather than winning arguments, we foster understanding and strengthen the bond with others.

Building Trust Through Authenticity

Authenticity plays a vital role in nurturing lasting relationships. We build trust with others when we are genuine and transparent in our interactions. Authenticity involves being true to ourselves while respecting the perspectives of those around us. By prioritizing honesty and integrity in our communications, we create a solid foundation for meaningful connections.

Cultivating Emotional Resilience

Emotional resilience is a valuable asset in both daily interactions and long-term relationships. It allows us to bounce back from setbacks, adapt to change, and maintain a positive outlook even in challenging circumstances. Cultivating emotional resilience involves embracing setbacks as learning opportunities, practicing self-care, and seeking support when needed.

Celebrating Successes Together

Lastly, *celebrating successes* strengthens bonds and fosters a sense of unity in relationships. Acknowledging big and small achievements demonstrates appreciation and reinforces positive behavior. By sharing joy and accomplishments with others, we create a supportive environment where everyone feels valued and encouraged.

Incorporating these strategies into your daily life can help you navigate social interactions more easily and foster deeper connections with those around you. By consistently applying EI insights, you can cultivate healthier relationships, enhance communication skills, and create a more harmonious environment for personal growth and fulfillment.

The emotional intelligence (EI) journey is an ongoing process that requires continuous learning and adaptation throughout our lives. Personal stories and practical examples are valuable tools in inspiring a commitment to lifelong growth in EI. By sharing experiences of triumphs and setbacks, individuals can see the power of resilience and the ability to overcome challenges through emotional understanding. *These narratives act as guiding lights, showcasing the real-life application of EI skills and their impact on relationships and personal well-being.*

Observing and making adjustments in our EI practice is crucial for long-term development. Just as Sarah learned from each interaction, we, too, can glean insights from our daily encounters to refine our emotional responses. By actively reflecting on our interactions, we can identify areas for improvement and make conscious efforts to adjust our behaviors accordingly. *This self-awareness is fundamental in the journey towards mastering emotional intelligence*

.

Personal stories of growth and transformation can serve as powerful motivators for individuals seeking to enhance their EI. Hearing how others have navigated challenging situations with grace and empathy can instill a sense of hope and determination in one's journey. *These stories remind us that growth is possible at any stage of life, encouraging us to embrace change and strive for emotional mastery.*

Practical examples offer tangible strategies for applying EI insights in everyday life. From managing conflict in the workplace to nurturing healthy relationships, these examples provide a roadmap for navigating complex emotional situations with clarity and compassion. By incorporating these strategies into our daily routines, we can cultivate a deeper understanding of ourselves and others, fostering harmonious connections.

Embracing a commitment to lifelong learning in emotional intelligence is not just about acquiring knowledge; it's about embodying empathy and understanding in all aspects of our lives.

Through ongoing observation, reflection, and adjustment, we can cultivate a more profound connection with our emotions and those of others. *This dedication to growth fosters a sense of personal fulfillment and enriches our interactions with the world around us*

.

The journey towards mastering emotional intelligence is a continuous evolution that unfolds through lived experiences. *By embracing this process wholeheartedly*, individuals can tap into their inner reservoirs of strength and resilience, transforming challenges into opportunities for growth. *Through ongoing observation, reflection, and adaptation*, we pave the way for deeper connections, enhanced relationships, and a more harmonious existence.

As we navigate the twists and turns of life's emotional landscape, let us remember that each moment presents a chance for growth and learning. *By staying committed to our emotional intelligence journey,* we enrich our lives and contribute positively to the world around us. *Embrace the power of continuous emotional learning,* for it is through this ongoing dedication that true transformation takes root.

Embracing the journey of emotional intelligence (EI) is not a one-time event but a lifelong commitment. Sarah's story and countless others shared in this book illustrate how everyday interactions are opportunities for growth and learning. By understanding and managing emotions effectively, we enhance our personal relationships and professional environments, leading to greater overall well-being.

Step-by-Step Process: Embracing Continuous Emotional Learning

Step 1: Commit to Lifelong Learning

Make a conscious decision to view EI as an evolving journey, not a final destination. Acknowledge that improvement is always possible, and embrace this mindset wholeheartedly.

Step 2: Set Goals for Emotional Growth

Identify which aspects of EI you wish to develop further. Set measurable objectives to enhance self-awareness, self-management, social awareness, and relationship management skills.

Step 3: Seek Opportunities for Emotional Learning

Actively pursue learning opportunities. Whether through workshops, books, or online communities, each resource offers unique insights that can deepen your understanding of EI.

Step 4: Reflect on Daily Interactions

Daily reflection on interactions helps pinpoint how emotions influence behavior and outcomes. This practice is crucial for recognizing patterns and planning strategic improvements in emotional responses.

Step 5: Practice Emotional Regulation Techniques

Incorporate techniques such as meditation or deep breathing into your routine. These practices aid in managing intense emotions and maintaining emotional equilibrium.

Step 6: Seek Feedback and Accountability

Feedback from peers and mentors is invaluable. Regular input can provide new perspectives on your emotional growth and areas needing attention.

Step 7: Adapt and Adjust

Stay flexible in your approach to EI. As you gain new insights and feedback, be prepared to adjust your strategies to better suit your growth needs.

By following these steps, you commit to a process of continuous improvement. Each step is designed to advance your emotional skills and integrate them seamlessly into all areas of life.

This book has equipped you with the knowledge and tools to embark on this transformative journey. Understanding and managing your emotions unlock the potential for significant personal and professional growth. Remember, the path to mastering emotional intelligence is continuous and filled with learning opportunities that enrich both relationships and individual well-being.

Embrace this journey with an open heart and mind, ready to explore the vast landscapes of emotional intelligence. Here's to your success in fostering deeper connections and achieving a harmonious life through the mastery of emotional intelligence.

Epilogue

Embracing the Journey Toward Emotional Mastery
As we conclude this exploration into emotional intelligence, it's essential to recognize that mastering our emotions is not merely an academic exercise; it's a vital component of living a fulfilling and harmonious life. This journey you've embarked upon is one of profound self-discovery and personal growth, one that can transform how you view yourself and interact with the world around you.

The principles and techniques shared in these pages are designed to be applied in real-world scenarios—at home, in the workplace, or within your social circles. From understanding the nuances of emotional awareness to mastering the skills of emotional regulation and empathy, each step you take is a building block towards a more resilient and emotionally intelligent self.

Recapitulating Key Insights

Throughout this book, we've tackled various facets of emotional intelligence. We started with the fundamentals of recognizing and naming our own emotions. Then, we delved into more complex territories like managing these emotions effectively and using them to foster better relationships. The strategies discussed—active listening, empathy exercises, and conflict resolution techniques—are your tools for lifelong use.

To truly benefit from these lessons, please keep practicing these skills regularly. Remember, emotional intelligence grows stronger with consistent effort and reflection. It's not about perfection; it's about progression.

Guidance for Continued Growth

Acknowledging that every individual's journey is unique, I suggest starting small. Please choose one or two techniques that resonate most with you and integrate them into your daily interactions.

Consider setting aside a few minutes daily to reflect on your emotional state or consciously applying empathy in conversations with others.

While this book strives to cover the essentials comprehensively, emotional intelligence is a vast field with ongoing research and evolving methodologies. Stay curious and continue exploring new studies and strategies to further enhance your understanding and application of EI.

A Call to Action

Let this not be the end but rather a new beginning in your quest for emotional mastery. Please take what you've learned and make it a living part of your identity. As you grow more adept at handling your emotions, you'll notice profound improvements in your relationships and professional life—opening doors to opportunities that align well with your enhanced capabilities.

A Lasting Impression

May your path be filled with learning, growth, and an ever-deepening understanding of yourself and others. Carry forward the torch of emotional awareness for personal gain and as a beacon for those around you.

"Emotions are not problems to be solved. They are signals to be interpreted." — Vironika Tugaleva.

This quote encapsulates our journey through emotional intelligence—a continuous process of interpreting and understanding our feelings and those of others for a more harmonious existence.

Reference for Embrace your Emotions

Capitalize The Power Of AI Copywriting | AllinWriter.com. https://allinwriter.com/blog/ai-copywriting/

History Project On Nationalism In India For Class 10th. https://hscprojects.com/history-project-on-nationalism-in-india-for-class-10th/

Embracing ADAS: The New Wave of Automotive Excellence - Domainyx Singular Domains. https://domainyx.com/embracing-adas-the-new-wave-of-automotive-excellence/

Emotions Unveiled: Navigating the Depths of Human Feelings | IOK STORE. https://www.iokstore.inkofknowledge.com/product-page/emotions-unveiled-navigating-the-depths-of-human-feelings

You Are Worthy Summit. https://myi.trenaboldenfieldscoaching.com/youareworthysummit2024

Decker, B., Landaeta, R., & Kotnour, T. (2009). Exploring the relationships between emotional intelligence and the use of knowledge transfer methods in the project environment. Knowledge Management Research & Practice. https://doi.org/10.1057/kmrp.2008.29

Law – Redditch United. http://www.redditchunited.com/category/law/

Mastering Emotional Intelligence at Work ðŸ€. https://simivalleyadultschool.org/blog/emotional-intelligence-at-work-guide

Leading Strategies From Leadership Coaching Experts – Cornell Review. https://www.cornellreview.org/general/leading-strategies-from-leadership-coaching-experts/

Bhati, R., Saraff, S., Bagchi, C., & Vijayarajan, V. (2018). Critical Decision Making Using Neural Networks. International Journal of Engineering & Technology. https://doi.org/10.14419/ijet.v7i4.10.20695

Mastering Self-Awareness for Personal Growth. https://lifecoachtraining.co/category/personal-development/mastering-self-awareness-for-personal-growth/

Associates & Affiliates: People Search Records | Glad I Know. https://giksitemaps.ironfly.bike/associates

From Darkness to Light | Journal. https://vocal.media/journal/from-darkness-to-light-npkn09qv

Ask Teri Lynn Blog: Empowering Women Through Therapy. https://www.askterilynn.com/post/ask-teri-lynn-blog-empowering-women-through-therapy

EMBRACING EMOTIONAL Intelligence: A Powerful Tool for Life - Touch Stone Publishers LTD. https://touchstonepublishers.com/embracing-emotional-intelligence-a-powerful-tool-for-life/

Elevate Leadership Skills | Mastering Emotional Intelligence. https://pearllemonacademy.com/mastering-emotional-intelligence-a-guide-for-executives/

Dispelling common myths about coaching. https://www.trueleadcoaching.com/post/dispelling-common-myths-about-coaching

Research - Emmanuel V. Dalavai. https://drevd.com/research/

Dr. Noha El Khouly: Mindset Mastery - Executive-Women. https://executive-women.me/dr-noha-el-khouly-mindset-mastery/

What Are The 7 Signs Of Emotional Intelligence. https://mormotivation.com/what-are-the-7-signs-of-emotional-intelligence/

What is the rarest DISC personality type? – Unleashing the Thrill of Flying Disc Sports. https://www.lancasterareafrisbeesports.com/what-is-the-rarest-disc-personality-type/

Best scannable fake ID code for fake ID deals: IDPAPA becomes industry leader overwhelming topfakeid. https://www.idpapa.org/Best-scannable-fake-id-idpapa-or-topfakeid

Why Gut Feelings Brain Connecting | Innovative Health Dallas. https://www.innovativehealthdallas.com/the-gut-feelings-brain-connection/

The Science of Emotional Intelligence in Boosting Team Productivity. https://digitalgyan.org/emotional-intelligence-in-boosting-productivity/

From Drab to Fab: How to Make Your Home More Stylish | The APKs. https://theapks.com/2023/03/14/from-drab-to-fab-how-to-make-your-home-more-stylish/

Amisha, B. (2024). Role of Emotional Intelligence in Leadership and Organizational Performance in Indonesia. International Journal of Psychology. https://doi.org/10.47604/ijp.2362

The Role of Emotional Intelligence in Successful Recruitment – AgileWPS. https://www.agilewps.com/the-role-of-emotional-intelligence-in-successful-recruitment/

Johanna Ulloa Giron on Emotional Intelligence and Its Pivotal Role in Personal and Professional Life – Journalism Online. https://www.journalismonline.com/johanna-ulloa-giron-on-emotional-intelligence-and-its-pivotal-role-in-personal-and-professional-life/

What is your level of emotional intelligence? - ProKensho. https://prokensho.com/what-is-your-level-of-emotional-intelligence/

Corporate Soft Skills Training Article. https://knowlesti.sg/corporate-soft-skills-training-article/

10 Ways Association Leaders Can Build Their Emotional Intelligence – Sidecar. https://sidecarglobal.com/leadership/

10-ways-association-leaders-can-build-their-emotional-intelligence/

Understanding Recursion: Unraveling the Mental Model of Self-Referential Loops - The Freedom Endeavour. https://thefreedomendeavour.com/recursion/

The Perfect Vacation | Stickman Bangkok. https://www.stickmanbangkok.com/readers-submissions/2005/09/the-perfect-vacation/

Kacmun - Everything You Need To Know!. https://www.todaypunch.com/kacmun/

The Art of Self-Revision: Coaching, Personal Narratives, and the Mastery – thinkingfeelingbeing.com. https://thinkingfeelingbeing.com/2024/01/19/the-art-of-self-revision-coaching-personal-narratives-and-the-mastery/

Top 2023 Port Huron Fitness and Yoga Influencers on Instagram: The Top 3. https://influencermarketing.ai/top-2023-port-huron-fitness-and-yoga-influencers-on-instagram-the-top-3/

Developing Leadership Presence With Emotional Intelligence - ESS Global Training Solutions. https://esoftskills.com/developing-leadership-presence-with-emotional-intelligence/

Lyashevsky, I. (2018). Teaching to Transfer in the Social Emotional Learning Context: The Case for an Instructional Model of the Human Emotion System. https://doi.org/10.7916/D8MP6KD6

Abu Qamar, S. Y., Alajjouri, S. N., Abu Okal, S. H., & Abu-Naser, S. S. (2023). Predicting the Number of Calories in a Dish Using Just Neural Network. https://core.ac.uk/download/590971543.pdf

The Crossroads of Innovation: The Complex AI Dilemma Can AI replace Human Intelligence?Man vs Tech. https://www.parliamentarysociety.com/post/the-crossroads-of-innovation-the-complex-ai-dilemma-can-ai-replace-human-intelligence-man-vs-tech

The Surprising Distinctions Between June and July Cancers - Which Zodiac Sign Are You? | Noodls. https://noodls.com/astrology/the-surprising-distinctions-between-june-and-july-cancers-which-zodiac-sign-are-you/

What Made Alexander the Great a Good Leader? 5 Highlights of His Leadership Evolution. https://icyheroes.com/what-made-alexander-the-great-a-good-leader/

Unit 3 Business Communication ATHE Level 3 Assignment Sample UK. https://www.diplomaassignmenthelp.co.uk/answers/unit-3-business-communication-athe-level-3-assignment-sample/

The Surprising Connection Between Mental Health and Wellness – Pulse Of The Blogosphere. https://coolacnetips.com/the-surprising-connection-between-mental-health-and-wellness/

Intelligence Theories, And Testing 2023. https://psychologyorg.com/intelligence-theories-and-testing-2023/

Emotional Intelligence Journal 2024 - Websetin. https://websetin.com/product/emotional-intelligence-journal

O'Brien, P., Bakarich, K., & Boyle, D. (2023). A Critical Look at Gender and Emotional Intelligence of Finance Professionals. Management Accounting Quarterly, 24(1), 14-21.

.   https://www.wisehead.coach/blog/how-to-improve-emotional-intelligence

Organizational Skills Training for Students with Attention Deficit Hyperactivity Disorder. https://graysonexecutivelearning.com/organizational-skills-training/

Emotional Journals - Just Perfect Health. https://www.jp-health.com/category/emotional-journals/

Self-Care Journaling Prompts: 55 Ideas For Self-Improvement - Ottos Journal. https://ottosjournal.com/self-care-journaling-prompts/

The Power of Emotional Intelligence: Building the Vibe Tribe - Slowerful. https://slowerful.com/the-power-of-emotional-intelligence-building-the-vibe-tribe/

Developing Emotional Intelligence – Geseron Employment Consulting Ltd.. https://geseronemploymentconsulting.com/products/developing-emotional-intelligence

The Role of Emotional Intelligence in Conflict Resolution - ESS Global Training Solutions. https://esoftskills.com/the-role-of-emotional-intelligence-in-conflict-resolution/

The Art of Empathy: Understanding Women's Thoughts and Feelings. https://borghi-teager.com/the-art-of-empathy-understanding-womens-thoughts-and-feelings/

Soulful Sunday : Unleashing Emotional Mastery – A Holistic Guide to Navigate Life's Rollercoaster – Digital Nomads Asia. https://digitalnomadsasia.com/2023/12/17/soulful-sunday-unleashing-emotional-mastery-a-holistic-guide-to-navigate-lifes-rollercoaster/

How Your Thoughts Influence Your Health and Well-being – Planet Ahd. https://planetahd.com/2023/health/how-your-thoughts-influence-your-health-and-well-being/

Work-life integration: Your well-being impacts your career. https://capital-placement.com/blog/work-life-integration/

The Power of Dialogue: Breaking Barriers and Encouraging Understanding - goodladworkshop. https://goodladworkshop.com/blog/the-power-of-dialogue-breaking-barriers-and-encouraging-understanding/

How can leaders build personal and professional resilience? - Pinpointing Potential. https://pinpointingpotential.com/blog/how-can-leaders-build-personal-and-professional-resilience/

Don't miss out!

Visit the website below and you can sign up to receive emails whenever Perry L. Davidson publishes a new book. There's no charge and no obligation.

https://books2read.com/r/B-A-UIWNB-WBFYD

BOOKS 2 READ

Connecting independent readers to independent writers.

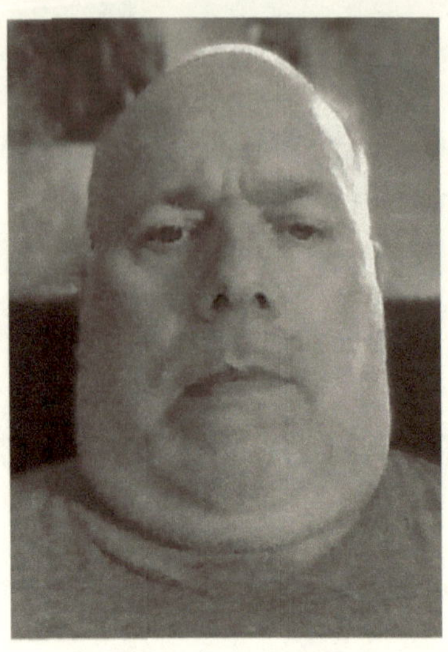

About the Author

At age 67, Perry L. Davidson is embarking on a journey that intertwines the culmination of a lifetime's experiences with fulfilling a long-held dream: publishing his first book. As a Navy veteran and a retired dispatcher, Perry L. Davidson brings a wealth of life experiences to his writing, which is marked by years of service, dedication, and a deep understanding of the human spirit.

Born and raised in Charleston, South Carolina, Perry L. Davidson spent his early years absorbing the stories and landscapes that would later become the backdrop for his narratives. His time in the Navy not only instilled in him a sense of discipline and resilience but also exposed him to a diversity of people and places, enriching his perspective and deepening his appreciation for the myriad ways in which life unfolds.

After his service, Perry L. Davidson transitioned to a career as a dispatcher. This role sharpened his ability to listen, empathize, and communicate effectively under pressure. These years were not just about managing crises but about understanding the stories behind each call. This experience honed his storytelling skills and fueled his passion for writing.

Now, in retirement, Perry L. Davidson has turned to the pen (or keyboard) as his tool for exploration and expression. His writing is a testament to his belief in the power of stories to connect, heal, and inspire. The themes of courage, perseverance, and the search for meaning that run through his work reflect his own life's journey.

Publishing his first book is a personal achievement for Perry L. Davidson and a gift to his readers. It offers insights and inspirations drawn from a well-lived life. As he steps into literature, he hopes to encourage others, regardless of age, to pursue their dreams and tell their stories, proving that it's always possible to start a new chapter.